Stopwatch

Student's Book & Workbook

4

Simon Brewster

Richmond

58 St Aldates
Oxford
OX1 1ST
United Kingdom

Stopwatch Student's Book Level 4

First Edition: March 2016
ISBN: 978-607-06-1242-8

© Text: Simon Brewster
© Richmond Publishing, S.A. de C.V. 2016
Av. Río Mixcoac No. 274, Col. Acacias,
Del. Benito Juárez, C.P. 03240, México, D.F.

Publisher: Justine Piekarowicz
Editorial Team: Suzanne Guerrero
Art and Design Coordinators: Karla Avila
Design: Karla Avila
Layout: Jaime Angeles, Karla Avila
Pre-Press Coordinator: Daniel Santillán
Pre-Press Team: Susana Alcántara, Virginia Arroyo
Cover Design: Karla Avila
Cover Photograph: © **Thinkstock.com** mezzotint (female sprinters start)

Illustrations: Ismael Vásquez pp. 16, 24, 31, 56, 57, 59, 87, 94, 99, 110, 122; Tomas Benitez pp. 28, 29, 44, 45; Fabian de Jesus Ramírez pp. 72, 78; Berenice Muñiz p. 59

Photographs: © **Shutterstock.com:** a katz p. 13 (bottom center), Karves p. 13 (top center), Mitch Gunn p. 13 (Inter players with the trophy), windmoon p. 13 (Lion Dance), a katz p. 14 (top right), Png Studio Photography p. 14 (School Marching Band), lev radin p. 16 (top right), Markus Gebauer p. 23 (bottom right), Valeriya Anufriyeva p. 34 (top center), Dietmar Temps p. 34 (Unidentified traditional healer), Jordi C p. 35 (members of a nigerian family), J. Henning Buchholz p. 48 (Sumo wrestler), Kasia Soszka p. 48 (Maneki-neko cat figurine), Tinxi p. 55 (take part in the Star Wars Parade), Aspen Photo p. 55 (cheer), Leonard Zhukovsky p. 55 (Novak Djokovic), robert cicchetti p. 55 (customers outside the Apple Store), cjmacer p. 56 (Lego minifigure businessman), Bubbers BB p. 56 (Lego minifigure Batman), hitch3r p. 56 (Wolf Hoffmann and Peter Baltes), Settawat Udom p. 58 (bottom left), Lauren Elisabeth p. 59 (top right), StonePhotos p. 61 (Union Pacific Freight Train), imranahmedsg p. 62 (Men playing cricket), JStone p. 62 (Malala), JASON TENCH p. 64 (championship banners), David Persson p. 64 (celebrates the Stanley cup victory), littleny p. 64 (Fans await entry), Matt Trommer p. 64 (pitcher), Kevin M. Kerfoot p. 65 (Museo De la Ciencia De Boston), Steve Lovegrove p. 67 (top left), Tinxi p. 68 (top right), Vania Georgieva p. 69 (roller coaster), Kenneth Sponsler p. 73 (Main Street), evantravels p. 76 (unidentified aborigines actor), Stanislav Fosenbauer p. 76 (ULURU KATA TJUTA NATIONAL PARK), Everett Collection p. 79 (Barack Obama), Denys Prykhodov p. 79 (iPad mini), Steven Collins p. 79 (ola gigante arrastra autos), Lucian Milasan p. 79 (London Olympics logo), Zeynep Demir p. 79 (iPhone 6), Oleg Golovnev p. 79 (Harry Potter), Tupungato p. 84 (La Rotonde restaurant), UKRID p. 84 (Cartoon Network Amazone), Ivan Garcia p. 84 (Oculus Rift), Paolo Bona p. 89 (AC Milan players), Aquarimage p. 89 (sailors sailing), Nikirov p. 89 (simulator skydiving glasses), peuceta p. 93 (musical group medieval), BlackMac p. 93 (Medieval parade), Vladimir Wrangel p. 93 (Medieval jousting), Sorbis p. 94 (Travelex counter) (train on RER station of Aeroport), Sean Locke Photography p. 95 (Opening Bottle), Maria_Janus p. 98 (Glacier), Dmitry Yashkin p. 98 (mountain bike), Centrill Media p. 103 (annual roundup of the State Park buffalo), Nila Newsom p. 109 (An auto rickshaws driving), 1000 Words p. 112 (A viewer browses Google Play store), Anton Bielousov p. 129 (Andre Luiz Moreira), p. 139 (bottom right), Anton_Ivanov p. 141 (logo Real Madrid), Marco Iacobucci EPP p. 141 (Real Madrid soccer team), Mehmet Cetin p. 142 (Sales Woman on the souvenir market), Alexey Boldin p. 148 (Google Gmail web page), filmlandscape p. 149 (bottom left), ZRyzner p. 149 (bottom center), Featureflash Photo Agency p. 153 (Surfer Bethany Hamilton), Brian A. Witkin p. 153 (Bethany Hamilton at the Super Girl Pro in Oceanside California), Gustavo Miguel Fernandes p. 153 (Bethany Hamilton in Rip Curl Pro 2010), Twin Design p. 154 (Avatar), Kaspars Grinvalds p. 156 (Netflix on the App Store), Everett Collection p. 157 (Ann Hathaway), Ovidiu Hrubaru p. 157 (Robert de Niro).
Images used under license from © **Shutterstock.com**

© **Wikipedia:** Creative Commons Attribution-Share Alike p. 63, Olav Bjaaland p. 105 (Roald Amundsen y sus compañeros mirando la bandera noruega), Illustreted London News p. 105 (A photograph of a dog team), Henry Bowers p. 105 (Pole party expedition), Abhinav Phangcho Choudhury (http://www.flickr.com/people/60354764@N03) p. 149 (Vagón de tren, India)

All rights reserved. No part of this work may be reproduced, stored in a retrieval system or transmitted in any form or by any means without prior written permission from the Publisher.

Richmond publications may contain links to third party websites or apps. We have no control over the content of these websites or apps, which may change frequently, and we are not responsible for the content or the way it may be used with our materials. Teachers and students are advised to exercise discretion when accessing the links.

The Publisher has made every effort to trace the owner of copyright material; however, the Publisher will correct any involuntary omission at the earliest opportunity.

Printed in Brazil

Printing and Finishing: PlenaPrint
Lot: 290941

Contents

Student's Book

- 4 — Scope and Sequence
- 7 — **Unit 0** Who are we?
- 13 — **Unit 1** What do you celebrate?
- 27 — **Unit 2** How are you feeling?
- 41 — **Unit 3** How can we save the planet?
- 55 — **Unit 4** What's your passion?
- 69 — **Unit 5** How much do you remember?
- 83 — **Unit 6** What do you need to travel?
- 97 — **Unit 7** How adventurous are you?
- 111 — **Unit 8** What do we have in common?

Workbook

- 126 — Unit 1
- 130 — Unit 2
- 134 — Unit 3
- 138 — Unit 4
- 142 — Unit 5
- 146 — Unit 6
- 150 — Unit 7
- 154 — Unit 8

- 158 — *Just for Fun* Answer Key
- 159 — Grammar Reference
- 168 — Verb List

Scope and Sequence

Unit	Vocabulary	Grammar	Skills
0 — Who are we?	**Review:** daily routines, food and drink, free-time activities, transportation **Parts of the Body**	Present simple; *Going to*; *Will*; Time expressions (present and future); Information questions with *wh-* words	**Listening:** Identifying statements and responses
1 — What do you celebrate?	**Celebrations:** birthday, blow out candles, get a diploma, graduation, Independence Day, make resolutions, New Year's Eve, open presents, set off fireworks, watch a parade, wave flags, wear a cap and gown	Present continuous (future meaning)	**Reading:** Making a mind map **Listening:** Understanding a description of a holiday **Project:** Making a holiday infographic
2 — How are you feeling?	**First Aid:** antiseptic spray, bandages, burn gel, first-aid kit, ice pack, medicine, thermometer **Symptoms and Injuries:** bruise, cut, fever, headache, runny nose, sore throat, stomachache, sunburn	*Should*; Short answers; Zero conditional	**Listening:** Taking notes to identify main points and supporting examples **Reading:** Reading a magazine article **Project:** Making a fact sheet
3 — How can we save the planet?	**The Environment:** conserve water, plant trees, pollute the environment, recycle, reduce carbon emissions, save electricity, send garbage to landfills, use clean energy, use fossil fuels	First conditional	**Reading:** Identifying opinions **Writing:** Giving reasons to support your opinions **Project:** Making a minidocumentary
4 — What's your passion?	**Fan Activities:** be a fan of, be good at, collect action figures, dress up as characters, get an autograph, put on face paint, put up posters, stand in line, wear a hat, wear team colors	Intensifiers; *Already, Yet*	**Reading:** Understanding questions in a dialogue **Speaking:** Asking questions as an active listener **Project:** Making a *Fan Activities* brochure

Unit	Vocabulary	Grammar	Skills
5 How much do you remember?	**Personal Experiences:** buy a lot of souvenirs, fall in love, forget, get in trouble, get lost, have a lot of fun, make a mistake, take care of **Keepsakes:** baby tooth, drawing, necklace, seashell, toy car	Past continuous; Short answers; Past continuous and past simple: *When*; Past continuous: *While*	**Reading:** Making connections between images and text **Listening:** Completing an outline **Project:** Making a personalized timeline
6 What do you need to travel?	**Travel:** book a flight, catch a train, exchange money, get a passport, hire a guide, pack a suitcase, stay in a hotel **Collocations:** get hot, get hungry, get lost, get ready, get started, get there, get thirsty, get up	Present perfect; Short answers; Present perfect: *Ever*; Present perfect: *Already, Yet*; *Been, Gone*	**Reading:** Reading images **Listening:** Identifying images from descriptions **Project:** Making a *Travel Experience* poster
7 How adventurous are you?	**Extreme Sports:** kite surfing, mountain biking, rock climbing, skydiving, snowboarding, white water rafting **Adjectives:** bored, boring, excited, exciting, interested, interesting, terrified, terrifying, thrilled, thrilling, tired, tiring	*Might*; *Would*; Present perfect: *Never*	**Reading:** Understanding text organization **Writing:** Classifying facts **Project:** Making an *Adventure Profile*
8 What do we have in common?	**Habits:** go out to eat, hang out, keep a journal, order take-out, sleep in, stay up late, stream movies, work out	*Too, Either*; *So, Neither*; *Me too, Me neither*	**Listening:** Identifying speakers **Reading:** Reading a blog **Project:** Conducting a *Social Acceptance* survey

Who are we?

Unit 0

1 Look and complete the descriptions of each person.

0. get up early – always
   yoga ❤
   ride her bike – every day
   bananas 🤢
   India

0. Pam always ____gets up early____. She likes to do ____yoga____ in the mornings. She ____rides her bike____ to school every day. She hates ____bananas____. Her dream is to travel to ____India____ in the future.

1. eat breakfast – never
   hang out with friends ❤❤
   walk – always
   carrots and lettuce 😐
   Rio de Janeiro

1. Betty _____.
   She loves to _____.
   She always _____ to school.
   She doesn't like _____.
   Her dream is to _____.

2. do homework – sometimes
   drawing ❤
   take a bus – often
   milk 😐
   Italy

2. Ben sometimes _____.
   He _____.
   He often _____.
   Ben doesn't _____.
   His dream _____.

3. go to the gym – often
   camping ❤❤
   go by car – always
   coffee 🤢
   Grand Canyon

3. Tom often _____.
   He _____.
   He _____ to school _____.
   Tom _____ coffee.
   _____.

2 Read and write the name of the person from Activity 1.

0. It's ten o'clock and I'm still in bed. I'm going to get up soon and have breakfast. I'm going to have some coffee to wake up and then I'm going to take a bus to my aunt's house. It's her birthday and I drew a picture for her.
   Ben

1. I'm here at the gym, but I hate it. I never come, but my mom says I have to exercise. I'm going to eat healthier, too. I always eat junk food. Well, my friends love me the way I am. I'm going to see them again tonight!
   _____

2. I'm walking my neighbors' dogs to **make** some **money**. I really want to travel next year. I am going to be ready then. Right now, my parents think I'm too young to travel **abroad** alone, especially to camp alone in the mountains!
   _____

3. I know I'm going to be the best instructor in the future! It's so relaxing to do this in my free time. Yes, standing on your head can be relaxing… And it exercises your **willpower**. I'm going to change completely. I'm going to do new things—maybe even eat bananas!
   _____

3 🎧¹ Listen and number the photos.

 0

4 🎧¹ Listen again and match.

0. It's cold in here. ——————————————— I'll bake her a cake.
1. What does your new dress look like? ———— I'll pick him up.
2. The school called. Robby is sick. —————— I'll try to see it on the weekend.
3. Mandy's birthday is tomorrow. ——————— I'll visit her this afternoon.
4. Grandma is lonely. ——————————————— I'll draw it for you.
5. It's a good movie. ——————————————— I'll close the window.

Guess What!
We use *will* to express immediate reactions to comments:
This bag is very heavy.
I **will** carry it for you.

Glossary
make money: earn money
abroad: a foreign country
willpower: determination and self-control

5 Look at the pictures and circle the main differences in their appearance.

6 Read the text and check. Then label the body parts.

> 10

Humans' closest relatives, the Neanderthals, lived in Europe and Asia during the Ice Age, about 200,000 to 30,000 years ago. They looked similar to us, but there were some differences in their **appearance**. They were shorter and more muscular than modern humans. This short and **stocky** stature was ideal for the cold weather because it consolidated heat. You can learn a lot about their activities just by looking at the remains of bones. One interesting thing is that their **arms** were **asymmetrical**: one arm was always stronger than the other, usually the right one. One of the possible reasons for this is that they spent a lot of time **scraping** animal skins, an activity that involves a lot of muscle work. Neanderthals also had really strong **hands**, ready to hunt and work. Their **legs** were short and strong and their **feet** quite big, which suggests that they walked and ran a lot. They were much more active than we are!

Neanderthals had flatter **heads** than us, but their **brains** were large, not small as many people thought. They had prominent **brow ridges** and their **cheekbones** were more angular. They had wider **noses** than humans and most Neanderthals had light **skin**. There is evidence that some Neanderthals had red **hair** and even **freckles**!

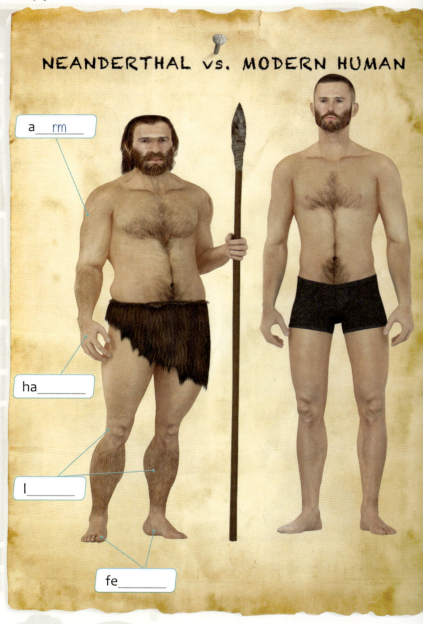

NEANDERTHAL vs. MODERN HUMAN

a__rm__
ha_____
l_____
fe_____

7 Read again and match the questions and answers.

0. Where did the Neanderthals live? — In Europe and Asia.
1. When did they live there? — During the Ice Age.
2. Did they look similar to modern humans? — Yes, they did.
3. Why were they short and stocky? — Because they needed more heat.
4. Were their brains smaller than ours? — No, they weren't.

Glossary
appearance: the way that someone or something looks
stocky: short and heavy; compact
asymmetrical: having two sides that are not the same; not symmetrical
scraping: removing (something) from a surface by rubbing an object or tool against it

8 🎧² Listen and circle the verbs you can hear.

9 Complete the sentences using the verbs from Activity 8.

0. Neanderthals _____used_____ sophisticated tools.
1. They _____ on cave walls.
2. They _____ their relatives in sickness.
3. Neanderthals _____ their dead.
4. They _____ music, too.

10 **Think Fast!** Change the sentences in Activity 9 into questions.

0. What _did Neanderthals use_____?
1. Where _____?
2. Who _____?
3. What _____?
4. Did _____?

Guess What!
One of the most surprising facts is that Neanderthals lived in Europe and Asia before humans. Neanderthals and humans both originated on the African continent, and scientists believe that for a period of time they both lived on Earth at the same time.

Vocabulary

1 Look at Lisa's scrapbook page and label the events.

Matt's graduation · Anna's birthday · Independence Day · New Year's Eve

2 Read and number the photo captions.

___ My cousin's **blowing out** her **candles**! I can't believe she's ten!

___ He's **wearing a cap and gown**. He looks really **handsome**.

___ We're **watching a parade**! This marching band is playing the **national anthem**.

___ She's **opening** her **presents**! That one was from me!

___ Here he's **getting a diploma**. He starts **college** in the fall.

___ Everyone's **waving** American **flags** and wearing red, white and blue!

___ I'm **making resolutions**. Next year, I want to eat better and smile more!

___ They're **setting off** fireworks. Beautiful!

Guess What!
On New Year's Eve in Denmark, people **smash** plates against their friends' doors for good luck in the next year.

3 Read and complete the celebration activities.

1. make _____
2. blow out _____
3. wear a _____
4. set off _____
5. wave _____
6. open _____
7. get a _____
8. watch a _____

4 🎧³ Listen and number the celebrations.

Independence Day ☐   a birthday ☐   New Year's Eve ☐   graduation ☐

5 Classify the words.

cake   candles   cap and gown   fireworks   flag   diploma   marching band   parade   presents   singing

Independence Day	Birthday	New Year's Eve	Graduation

6 Think Fast! Scramble five celebrations words for a classmate to guess.

Glossary

handsome: good-looking

national anthem: the official song of a country

college: a school where you go after high school to get a bachelor's degree

smash: to break

Grammar

1 Read quickly and complete.

Thanksgiving is one of the largest celebrations in the United States. It is always on the fourth Thursday of November. Millions of people gather for a day of feasting, football and family. On Thanksgiving morning, 3.5 million people watch the Macy's Thanksgiving Day Parade in New York City. More than 50 million people watch the event on TV. In the afternoon or evening, families have a delicious turkey dinner.

Every year, millions of people celebrate _____ by watching the _____ _____ in New York City.

turkey · mashed potatoes · cranberry sauce · stuffing

2 Read and circle the correct option.

1. Thanksgiving is **today** / **next week**.
2. They **are** / **aren't** celebrating Thanksgiving in New York.
3. They **are** / **aren't** visiting their grandparents next week.

Guess What! Pumpkin pie is the most popular pie for Thanksgiving dinners.

WE'RE VISITING GRANDPARENTS NEXT WEEK!

...WHICH MEANS WE'RE CELEBRATING THANKSGIVING IN NEW YORK THIS YEAR!

HOORAY! WHEN ARE WE LEAVING?

Happy Thanksgiving

Present Continuous (future meaning)

We can use Present Continuous to talk about future plans, such as a travel itinerary.

3 🎧⁴ **Listen and mark (✓ or ✗) the plans for the trip.**

✈️ flying ☐   🚌 taking the bus ☐

🧳 staying in a hotel ☐   staying with their grandparents ☐

🍗 having dinner ☐   🏈 watching football ☐

🌙 going shopping at midnight ☐   🚩 going to the parade ☐

4 🎧⁵ **Listen and circle T (True) or F (False).**

1. The kids are arriving tomorrow morning. — T F
2. Grandma is baking a pie this afternoon. — T F
3. She's cooking the turkey on Thursday. — T F
4. Grandpa isn't helping with the preparations. — T F
5. He's taking the grandkids to the parade. — T F

5 🎧⁵ **Listen again and unscramble the sentences.**

1. are / when / coming / the kids

   _____?

2. not / I / making / a pie / am

   _____.

3. you / taking / the kids / to / are / the parade

   _____.

4. cooking / the turkey / on Thursday / am / I

   _____.

6 **Think Fast!** In your notebook, write five sentences about Stickman's plans for Thanksgiving.
(3 min)

Glossary

bakery: a store where you can buy bread, cake, cookies or pies

nap: a short sleep during the day

Reading & Listening

1 Read and circle the correct option.

Religious Celebrations

All over the world, religious celebrations are important to billions of people! Here are two religious celebrations: bar and bat mitzvahs and Eid al-Fitr.

Bar and Bat Mitzvahs

In the Jewish community, a boy becomes a bar mitzvah when he turns 13. (A bat mitzvah is a similar ceremony for girls when they turn 12.) This event celebrates the transition to **adulthood**. As a part of the occasion, children **recite** religious texts. After this ceremony, the bar or bat mitzvah receives gifts and money in multiples of 18—a number that symbolizes a long life. From this time on, they can participate as adults in religious activities.

Eid al-Fitr

Eid al-Fitr (pronounced ed œl fIt-Ur) is an important religious holiday for the world's two billion Muslims. Eid al-Fitr, or Eid, is the first day after Ramadan, a month of **fasting**. On this day, Muslims say **prayers** and have a special meal. Children open presents. Many people give to the poor or donate money to charities, an important part of the religion.

1. Bar and bat mitzvahs are **Jewish** / **Muslim** celebrations.
2. A *bar mitzvah* is the name of a celebration and the **boy** / **girl** who participates.
3. In a bat mitzvah, the participant is **12** / **13**.
4. The number **12** / **18** represents long life.
5. Eid al-Fitr is a **Jewish** / **Muslim** celebration.
6. Eid occurs **before** / **after** Ramadan.
7. People celebrate Eid by **fasting** / **eating**.

 **Be Strategic!**
Making a mind map can help you to understand and remember information from a text. Identify the topics and then add details.

2 Read again and complete the mind map in your notebook.

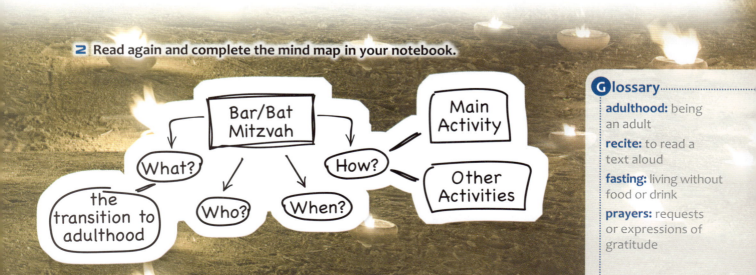

Glossary
adulthood: being an adult
recite: to read a text aloud
fasting: living without food or drink
prayers: requests or expressions of gratitude

3 🎧⁶ **Listen and number.**

Wesak is a religious celebration, so many Buddhists go to a temple to pray and meditate. They often take flowers and _____ with them. ☐

And in general, when we celebrate Wesak Day, we try to make other people _____, especially people who are poor or sick. ☐

Sunisa here! It's May and next week is a very special holiday in Thailand, and for Buddhists all over the _____: Wesak Day! On Wesak, we celebrate the **birth**, the **enlightenment** and the **death** of Buddha. ☐

At the temple, people give _____ to the Buddhist monks—men who devote themselves to a simple life (they're easy to identify because they wear **robes**). At night, everyone walks around the temple _____ times in a special ceremony. ☐

4 🎧⁶ **Listen again and complete.**

5 In your notebook, make a mind map for Wesak Day.

Stop and Think! What do you know about religious celebrations around the world?

Glossary
- **birth:** when a person is born
- **enlightenment:** spiritual awakening
- **death:** when a person dies
- **robes:** long, loose gowns

Culture

1 Read the facts about Mexico and underline the one you find the most interesting.

Did you know...

In 2015, nearly 26 million tourists visited Mexico.

Mexico has 11 active volcanoes.

The largest pyramid in the world is in Cholula, in the Mexican state of Puebla.

Foods like red tomato, corn, avocado and chocolate originated in Mexico.

The smallest dog **breed** in the world, the chihuahua, got its name after the State of Chihuahua in northern Mexico.

Every year, millions of monarch butterflies travel to Mexico from the US and Canada.

There are 32 UNESCO world heritage sites in Mexico.

2 Read and label.

Why?   Who?   When?   Main Activities   Other Activities

 November 1st and 2nd

 creating an *ofrenda*: a display with *pan de muerto*—"bread of the dead," sugar skulls, candles and flowers

 visiting **graves** in a **cemetery** (Some people stay all night!)

 decorating homes and public spaces with *calacas*

 people in Mexico: families, schools

 to remember to people who have died

LA CATRINA

La Catrina is one of the most popular symbols of the Day of the Dead in Mexico. What is *La Catrina*? It's a skeleton of a woman in an elegant hat and a long formal dress.

La Catrina is the invention of a famous Mexican illustrator, Jose Guadalupe Posada, just before the Mexican Revolution. He drew La Catrina in 1910 to make fun of **wealthy** Mexicans who imitated European styles. Posada took his inspiration from Mictecacihuatl (mIk-tEk-si-wa-t´l), the Aztec goddess of death and queen of the underworld. Posada only illustrated the head of La Catrina in 1910. In 1947, the Mexican artist Diego Rivera painted a full-length view of La Catrina in the mural *"Dream of a Sunday Afternoon in Alameda Park."*

Nowadays, some people wear costumes to look like La Catrina, even outside of Mexico.

▲ *La Catrina*, by Jose Guadalupe Posada

3 Read and answer in your notebook.
1. What is *La Catrina*?
2. When did Jose Guadalupe Posada invent this figure?
3. Why did he draw this figure wearing an elegant hat?
4. Who is Mictecacihuatl?
5. How was Diego Rivera's Catrina different?

Stop and Think! How can holidays bring people together as a community?

Glossary

breed: a type of dog with specific characteristics

graves: tombs; spaces for dead people in a cemetery

cemetery: an area with tombs

wealthy: rich

Project

1 Look at the St. Patrick's Day infographic on page 23. Read and match.

1. St. Patrick is the patron of this country.   Murphy
2. This plant is a symbol of Ireland.   Boston
3. This is a common Irish surname.   leprechaun
4. The first St. Patrick's Day parade was here.   Ireland
5. These are Irish instruments.   Australia
6. This is a magical creature.   shamrock
7. People celebrate St. Patrick's Day here too.   bagpipes

2 🎧⁷ Listen and complete the sentences.

1. Shaun's surname is _____.
2. He lives in _____.
3. His family is originally from _____.
4. There's a big _____ and fireworks in Sydney on St. Patrick's Day.
5. This year his family is having a _____ with Irish music and dancing.

3 Choose and research another celebration's origins and traditions.

Halloween

Hanukkah

Groundhog Day

Mardi Gras

Easter

Memorial Day

4 Make an infographic with your findings. Add a party invitation to your infographic.

We're organizing a St. Patrick's Day party at school on March 17th at 7:30 p.m.

Wear something green!

We're having Irish dancing and music.

See you there!

Happy St. Patrick's Day

St. Patrick is the patron saint of Ireland.

17 March — St. Patrick's Day is March 17. According to tradition, this is the date of St. Patrick's death.

387	403	409	432	461
Patrick was born in Roman England.	Pirates kidnapped Patrick and took him to Ireland as a slave.	Patrick escaped and returned to England.	Patrick went to Ireland to teach Christianity.	Patrick died.

The shamrock—a common three-leafed plant in Ireland—is a symbol of Ireland and St. Patrick's Day. St. Patrick used the shamrock to teach about his religion.

St. Patrick's Day is special to people with Irish ancestors. Common Irish surnames include Murphy, Kelly, O'Brien, Ryan, O'Neill and O'Connor.

90% of Americans celebrate St. Patrick's Day! In the US, you can buy green "shamrock" milkshakes on St. Patrick's Day. In Chicago, they dye the river green to celebrate this day.

Many people dress as leprechauns for St. Patrick's Day. A leprechaun is a kind of magical creature: a little man with a beard dressed in green clothing.

The very first St. Patrick's Day parade was not in Ireland but in Boston in **1737.**

Even people in Australia celebrate St. Patrick's Day! St. Patrick's Day parades normally include people playing bagpipes, a traditional Irish instrument.

Review

1 Look and label the celebrations.

_____ _____

_____ _____

2 Read and match. Then look and number the scenes.

1. blow out   2. get a cap and gown
   candles   a parade
3. set off   4. make flags
   a diploma   fireworks
                        presents
6. watch   5. wear
   resolutions
7. wave   8. open

3 Unscramble the sentences.

1. you / what / doing / after / school / are / ?
   _____

2. is / Janice / party / not / going / the / to
   _____

3. we / giving / sweater / for / Tim / birthday / a / his / are
   _____

4. to / you / the / going / football / are / tonight / game / ?
   _____

5. parents / are / my / having / not / for / Thanksgiving / turkey
   _____

4 Complete the e-mail using the correct forms of the verbs.

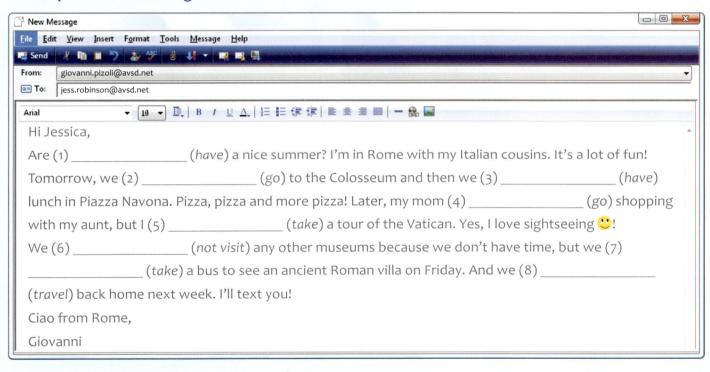

Hi Jessica,

Are (1) _____ (have) a nice summer? I'm in Rome with my Italian cousins. It's a lot of fun! Tomorrow, we (2) _____ (go) to the Colosseum and then we (3) _____ (have) lunch in Piazza Navona. Pizza, pizza and more pizza! Later, my mom (4) _____ (go) shopping with my aunt, but I (5) _____ (take) a tour of the Vatican. Yes, I love sightseeing 🙂! We (6) _____ (not visit) any other museums because we don't have time, but we (7) _____ (take) a bus to see an ancient Roman villa on Friday. And we (8) _____ (travel) back home next week. I'll text you!

Ciao from Rome,

Giovanni

5 Rewrite the sentences.

1. We're going to a rock concert tonight! → ?
   _____

2. My friend Amy's going to the parade. → –
   _____

3. We aren't setting off fireworks tonight. → +
   _____

4. Is Paul having a graduation party? → +
   _____

5. You're going to the party. → ?
   _____

Just for Fun

1 Read and guess the holiday. Unscramble and write.

1 EWHALONLE

"Tonight we're visiting houses in our neighborhood. I'm wearing a vampire costume. I hope I get a lot of candy!"

2 EANDPENDIDEN YCE

"We decorated our house with flags. Today we're watching a parade. In the afternoon, we're having a picnic. At night, we're setting off fireworks!"

3 ANEENYLTI'A DVS

"Some people send flowers or buy expensive gifts. My friends and I are exchanging candy and cards."

4 VIKINGSHANTG

"In my family… we're watching a parade in the morning. Then we're eating an enormous meal. On Friday, we're going shopping!"

2 Read and solve the puzzle.

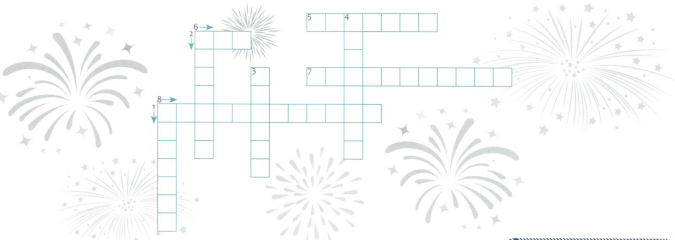

Down ↓
1. a skeleton in a dress
2. lights on a birthday cake
3. a popular food on Thanksgiving
4. gifts people receive

Across →
5. a document you receive at graduation
6. a square hat for graduation
7. decisions for the New Year
8. holidays or special occasions

Guess What!
Finland has a wife-carrying festival! It's a race! Husbands carry their wives through a 235-meter obstacle course.

Vocabulary

1 🎧⁸ Listen and number the items.

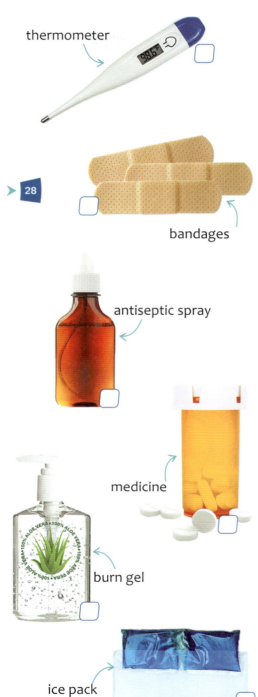

thermometer

bandages

antiseptic spray

medicine

burn gel

ice pack

first-aid kit

2 Read the comic and label the symptoms and injuries.

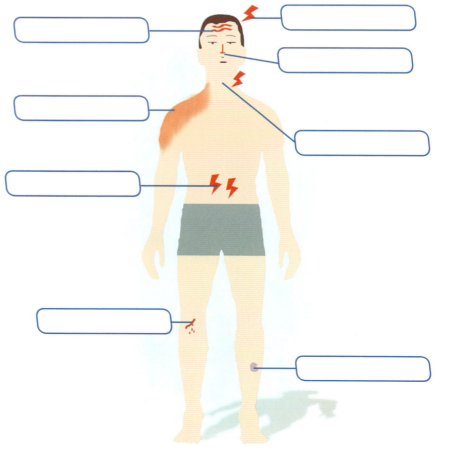

3 Look and suggest what to use in each case.

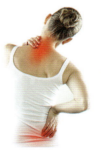

_____ _____ _____

_____ _____ _____

4 Think Fast! Write two examples for each category in your notebook.

Symptoms   Injuries   First Aid

1 Rate the health factors. How do they affect a person's health?

dangerous 0 1 2 3 4 5 6 7 8 9 10 very beneficial

1. exercising
2. smoking cigarettes
3. drinking soda
4. going to bed late
5. being stressed out
6. listening to loud music
7. eating a balanced diet
8. reducing screen time

2 🎧⁹ Listen and number the recommendations.

wear a seatbelt

wear a helmet

turn down the volume

get enough sleep

3 Look and answer with a classmate.

Is it OK to drink soda?

Should I stop checking Facebook in bed?

What kind of exercise should I do?

How much sleep should I get?

What should I include in my diet?

How much water should I drink?

Should

We use *should* for advice and recommendations:
You **should** exercise junk food.
You **shouldn't** eat junk food.

Guess What!
We often use *you* to talk about people in general: **You** shouldn't eat cake for breakfast.

Zero Conditional

These sentences express facts using Present Simple. You can use *if* or *when* to express the condition.

4 Read the sentences. Circle the conditions and then underline the consequences.

1. When you reduce your screen time, you have more time for other activities.
2. You can avoid many health problems if you eat a balanced diet.

5 Read the examples in Activity 4. Then circle *T* (True) or *F* (False).

1. The condition always comes before the consequence.   T   F
2. *If* and *when* have the same meaning in conditionals.   T   F
3. You need a comma (,) after the consequence.   T   F
4. You use the Present Simple in the condition.   T   F
5. You use the Present Simple in the consequence.   T   F

6 Complete the sentences.

1. you drink water / your digestion is better

   When _____.

2. you don't sleep enough / you feel terrible

   If _____.

3. you look at a screen too long / you can't fall asleep

   When _____.

4. you eat well / you feel better

   If _____.

7 Think Fast! In your notebook, rewrite the sentences in Activity 6. Put the consequence first in each sentence.

Listening and Reading

1 Look and discuss with a classmate. What makes you happy?

caring about others ☐   good food ☐

money ☐   community ☐

exercise ☐   sunshine ☐

music ☐   pets ☐

relaxation ☐   positive thinking ☐

Be Strategic! Taking notes can help you to distinguish between main points and supporting examples.

2 🎧¹⁰ Listen and mark (✓) the topics you hear.

3 🎧¹⁰ Listen again and add the topics from Activity 2 to the chart. Then complete the examples.

Happiness Factors	Examples
1.	_____, _____, **strangers**
2.	_____, gratitude and kindness
3.	going to the gym, playing _____ or taking a _____
4.	a _____, a _____, a _____
5.	going to a **festival**, joining a _____, _____

Guess What! According to the United Nation's World Happiness Report, Denmark is the happiest country in the world followed by Norway, Switzerland and the Netherlands.

4 Read and choose the best option.

The article explains how to be kind and optimistic. ☐

The article explains how to focus on the present moment. ☐

The article gives a few techniques for relaxation. ☐

How mindful are you?

Breathe in… Breathe out… Focus only on your breathing…. Breathe in… Breathe out… But your mind is somewhere else! You're thinking about a test… or an argument with a friend. You're wondering if you have any messages. Maybe you're hungry for a snack or imagining your afternoon routine. LOTS of things can distract us—**regrets** about the past or **worries** about the future—and we forget to see and feel and listen. Mindfulness is the opposite of that.

When you're mindful, you actively focus on the present moment. Mindfulness is experiencing the world in high definition! What is your body doing? What are your thoughts? What is happening around you? And when you're mindful, you suspend criticism. Be aware of your thoughts. Observe them.

"Mindfulness" has its origins in ancient Buddhism, but it isn't necessary to be Buddhist to practice mindfulness. In fact, many schools offer classes in mindfulness and meditation. It improves your health and memory. It reduces stress, too. Do you want to try it? Here's a technique to practice: Observe a raisin. Look at it carefully. Look at every detail. How does it feel in your hand? **Notice** its weight. Try to observe everything about the raisin. Then eat the raisin as slowly as possible. What do you notice? What sensations do you experience?

Now, imagine if you eat everything in this way. Imagine that in a conversation, you notice the details in a person's expression. Every time you go outside, you feel the air touch your face and notice the sound of your footsteps. It is a simple exercise, but it can improve your life!

5 Read again and complete.

1. Mindfulness focuses on the _____.
2. _____ often distract us from noticing the world around us.
3. One of the techniques to stay mindful is to _____.
4. Mindfulness can improve _____ and _____.

Stop and Think! How can being mindful help you be happy?

Glossary

strangers: people you don't know

festival: a community celebration

regrets: negative feelings about the past; guilt

worries: (sing. worry) anxiety about the future

notice: see; pay attention to

Culture

1 Read and circle the correct option. Then check the answers below.

1. There are _____ countries in Africa.
   a) 14
   b) 42
   c) 54

2. The most common language in Africa is _____
   a) English.
   b) Arabic.
   c) Swahili.

3. The largest city in Africa is _____
   a) Johannesburg, South Africa.
   b) Cairo, Egypt.
   c) Lagos, Nigeria.

4. In 1967, the first heart **transplant** took place in _____
   a) Kenya.
   b) South Africa.
   c) Nigeria.

5. Rhinos are in danger because people in _____ believe that their horns have medicinal properties.
   a) America
   b) Europe
   c) Asia

Answers: 1. 54, 2. English, 3. Lagos, 4. South Africa, 5. Asia

2 Read and number.

1. A Traditional African Medicine
2. Traditional **Healers**
3. **Healthcare** in Africa
4. Healers and Modern Medicine

In some parts of Africa, a plant called *buchu* is a popular medicine. It can treat infections. People sometimes use the leaves to make tea.

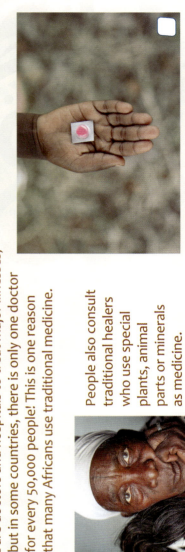

Some healers also have **training** in modern medicine. They can identify symptoms of diseases such as tuberculosis and HIV/AIDS. Healers can send people with these **diseases** to a doctor to get medication.

In Africa, healthcare comes in many forms. There are doctors and hospitals to treat major illnesses, but in some countries, there is only one doctor for every 50,000 people! This is one reason that many Africans use traditional medicine.

People also consult traditional healers who use special plants, animal parts or minerals as medicine. Sometimes they treat people by doing dances. Many people trust healers more than doctors.

34

3 Read again and match.

1. Traditional medicine — is a medicinal plant.
2. Some countries — modern medicine.
3. Buchu — is very common.
4. Healers use — are diseases.
5. Some healers learn — plants, animal parts or minerals.
6. Tuberculosis and HIV/AIDS — have few doctors.

4 🎧 11 Listen and circle T (True) or F (False).

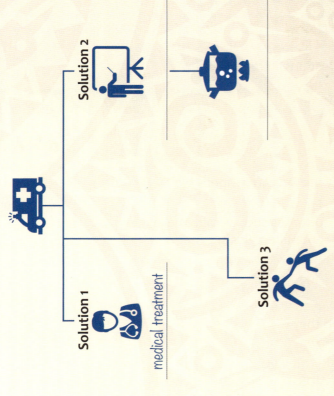

1. Blessing Kwomo is a doctor. T F
2. She is from South Africa. T F
3. The De Rehoboths Therapeutic Studio helps families prevent diseases. T F
4. They provide transportation to clinics and hospitals. T F
5. They provide medical treatment and health education. T F
6. They give money to the patients. T F

5 🎧 11 Listen again and complete.

Problem: Patients get sick again after treatment.

Solution 1 — medical treatment

Solution 2

Solution 3

Glossary

transplant: an operation to replace an organ
healers: people who are experts in the use of traditional medicine
healthcare: medical care
training: instruction
diseases: severe illnesses
entrepreneur: a person who starts a business

Stop and Think! What do you do to stay healthy?

1 Read and complete the fact sheet.

cause   clean   hands   illnesses   infectious   transmitted

INFECTIOUS DISEASES

Symptoms

- fever
- diarrhea
- muscle pain
- coughing

Causes

Bacteria are responsible for _____ diseases such as salmonella and tuberculosis.

Viruses are smaller than bacteria and they cause a multitude of _____: colds, the flu and even AIDS.

Fungi _____ skin diseases, such as athlete's foot. Fungi can also infect your lungs or nervous system.

Parasites cause many diseases. Malaria is caused by a parasite that is _____ by mosquitoes.

Prevention

- Wash your _____ frequently.
- Wash fruits and vegetables.
- Cook food thoroughly.
- Drink _____ water.
- Get vaccinations.

2 Read the fact sheet about Chikungunya on page 37. Then answer the questions.

1. What are the symptoms of Chikungunya?
   _____

2. What causes the disease?
   _____

3. How can you prevent it?
   _____

3 Make a fact sheet about an infectious disease.

1. Include sections for symptoms, causes and prevention.
2. Include other important facts: countries, number of cases, etc.

CHIKUNGUNYA

CAUSES

What **causes** Chikungunya? Chikungunya is caused by **a virus**.

Mosquitoes transmit this virus.

It is present in **45** countries.

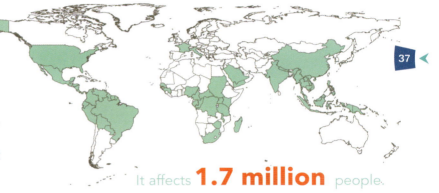

It affects **1.7 million** people.

SYMPTOMS

Chikungunya is characterized by fever and pain in the joints. Other symptoms may include headache, muscle pain, joint swelling or a rash.

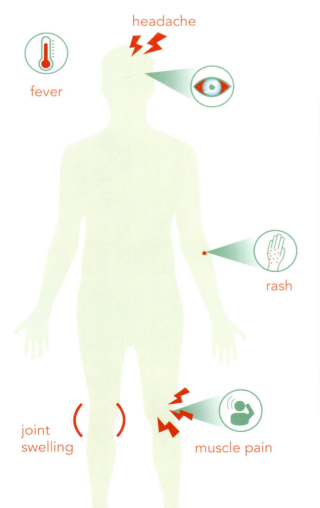

- fever
- headache
- rash
- joint swelling
- muscle pain

PREVENTION

There is **no** vaccine for Chikungunya. You prevent Chikungunya by preventing **mosquito** bites.

 Use mosquito repellant.

 Use mosquito nets.

 Empty water containers where mosquitoes reproduce.

 In some regions, people prevent Chikungunya by having a pet fish in their water containers. The fish eats the mosquito larvae and prevents the transmission of diseases!

Review

1 Read and match.

1. antiseptic spray — a substance for skin damage caused by the sun or something hot
2. burn gel — something you take to treat an illness
3. bandages — a very cold bag to put on an injury
4. first aid kit — an instrument for measuring temperature
5. ice pack — a substance for preventing infection
6. medicine — a box or bag containing medicines, creams and bandages
7. thermometer — a strip of cloth or plastic to cover an injury

2 Find and circle eight words for symptoms and injuries.

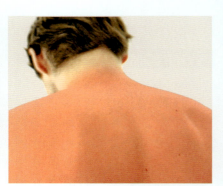

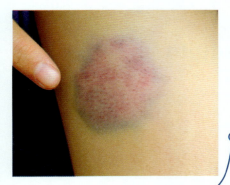

```
I F C B P B H I E T B W T
L I E Q R R I J A R E E E
N M G U O K M O K T C H U
B D I H E C R O U U J C U
Y S A U Z H R E V E F A S
E A B E T C Q O Z F E H U
H U Y E C G A K P Q O C N
D E R U N N Y N O S E A B
D O A E C F N K J W J M U
S S U D B T M O Y T H O R
F T E I A L U C E J E T N
O G X V V C H C M F N S U
T E C E S J H R F O K E F
K R R X J V L E B R T J P
```

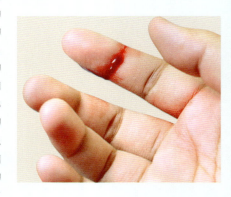

3 **Write sentences using *should* and *shouldn't*.**

 eat candy for breakfast

 brush your teeth after every meal

 exercise regularly

 watch TV for six hours every day

1. _____
2. _____
3. _____
4. _____

4 **Read and underline the consequence.**
1. If you eat more vegetables, you reduce your risk of disease.
2. It's easier to lose weight if you stop drinking soda.
3. When you meditate, you forget about worries and regrets.
4. People are happier when they practice positive thinking.

5 **Correct the sentences.**
1. You gain weight when you to consume a lot of calories.
   _____
2. When you burn calories, you exercise.
   _____
3. When you're breaking a bone, it takes six weeks to heal.
   _____
4. If you didn't drink enough water, you become dehydrated.
   _____
5. If you get sick, you don't wash your hands regularly.
   _____

Just for Fun

1 Take the trivia quiz. Read and circle *T* (True) or *F* (False). Then check your answers on page 158.

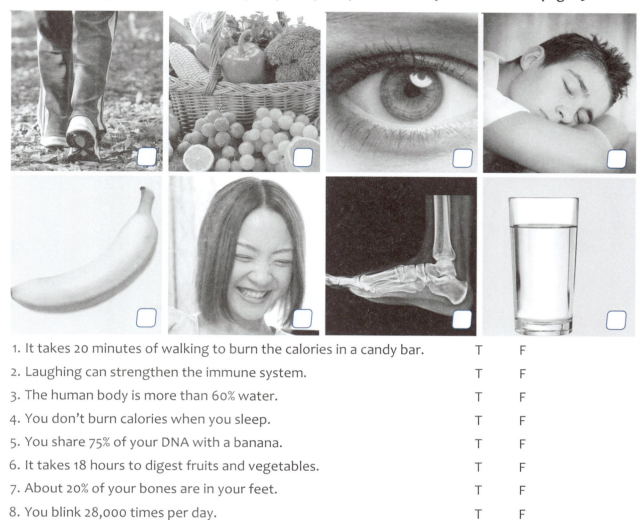

1. It takes 20 minutes of walking to burn the calories in a candy bar.   T   F
2. Laughing can strengthen the immune system.   T   F
3. The human body is more than 60% water.   T   F
4. You don't burn calories when you sleep.   T   F
5. You share 75% of your DNA with a banana.   T   F
6. It takes 18 hours to digest fruits and vegetables.   T   F
7. About 20% of your bones are in your feet.   T   F
8. You blink 28,000 times per day.   T   F

2 Read again and number the photos. Then underline the fact that surprised you the most.

3 Read the proverbs. Do you agree?

 Early to bed, early to rise makes a man healthy, wealthy and wise.

 Seven days without exercise makes one weak.

 An apple a day keeps the doctor away.

 You are what you eat.

 Prevention is better than cure.

 Health is wealth.

How can we save the planet?
3

Vocabulary

Create Awareness

Know Your Footprint
Carbon dioxide, or CO2, is a gas in our atmosphere. Too much CO2 can cause severe changes in our planet's climate! **Reduce carbon emissions** today!

Use Less Fuel
Most vehicles **use fossil fuels** and produce a lot of CO2. Take the bus or **carpool**—it's more efficient!

Conserve Water
Take short showers and don't use more water than necessary.

Save Electricity
Most **power plants** generate electricity using fossil fuels. Save electricity by turning off lights and appliances when you aren't using them.

Plant Trees
Trees absorb carbon dioxide, protect the **soil** and keep temperatures cooler in the summer. Plant one today!

Use Clean Energy
Solar panels and wind turbines don't **pollute the environment**.

---

1 Look and circle the correct option.

1. conserve water / pollute the environment

2. use fossil fuels / plant trees

3. recycle / send garbage to landfills

4. save electricity / use clean energy

2 Complete the phrases and answer. Which actions help the environment?

1. _____ trees
2. _____ electricity
3. _____ the environment
4. _____ your carbon footprint
5. conserve _____
6. send garbage to _____
7. use clean _____
8. use fossil _____

42

Recycle

Where does your garbage go? Every day, cities **send** tons of **garbage to landfills**. But many materials shouldn't go there—they can be used again. Recycle paper, plastic, **glass** and metal.

3 Match the verbs with the definitions.

1. conserve — to protect a natural resource
2. save — to introduce garbage and chemicals to a place
3. recycle — to put something in the ground to grow
4. pollute — to use less of something
5. plant — to transform objects into new things

4 🎧12 Listen and number the suggestions.

 ☐ Eat less meat. ☐ Wear a sweater.

 ☐ Buy a new car. ☐ Read a book.

5 Think Fast! Read and mark (✓) about you. Then calculate your score.

How much do you care about the environment?

	Always (+5)	Sometimes (+3)	Never (0)
1. I use public transportation.			
2. I use only the water that I need.			
3. I recycle plastic, glass, metal and paper.			
4. I save energy by turning off lights.			
5. My family uses modern lightbulbs.			
6. We sort our trash at home.			

Scores: 24–30 points → Awesome! / 15–23 points → Not bad! / 0–15 → Try a little harder!

Guess What!

Fossil fuels like oil and gas come from plants that were alive millions of years ago!

Glossary

carpool: to arrange to travel together in the same car
power plants: factories that generate electricity
soil: earth; dirt
glass: a hard transparent material

Grammar

1 Look at the picture and mark (✓) the actions that help the environment and (✗) actions that pollute the environment.

2 Read the *Ask Miss Eco* column and underline the four environmental problems.

Ask Miss Eco

Hi. My mom says I should pick up after my dog. I don't understand what harm it does. If I don't clean it, what will happen? (Danny 14)

Your mom's right, Danny. Dog poop not only smells, it contains parasites and can cause infections in humans and animals. It also pollutes water. If more people pick up after their dogs, the city will be much cleaner. As a dog owner, it's your responsibility!

Someone told me that noise pollution can cause physical damage. What will happen if I listen to loud music? (Carol, 15)

If you listen to loud music, especially with headphones on, you will have permanent hearing problems by the age of 40. There is already a lot of noise around you—planes, cars, motorcycles, radios and heavy machinery—these all cause noise pollution.

I heard the term "light pollution." Does this kind of pollution really exist? (Theo, 13)

That's an interesting question, Theo. Light pollution does exist. There are more and more lights everywhere. Artificial lights in towns and cities stop us from having a clear view of the sky. If we use lights everywhere, we will soon forget what a starry sky is!

If I take a shower every day, will I use less water than if I take a bath? (Olivia, 14)

That is correct, Olivia. You use 26 liters of water for a quick shower and about 94 liters of water for a bath. You will always use less water if you take showers than if you take a bath. But don't stay in the shower for more than 10 minutes!

What are the main causes of air pollution and what can I do? (Sean, 16)

Where do I start? Air pollution is caused mainly by emissions from factories and from burning fossil fuels like coal and gasoline. Cars produce a lot of bad gases, which causes air pollution. The next time your father or mother takes you to school, make sure you take a friend or two. If we share our cars, there will be fewer cars in the streets and less pollution in the air!

First Conditional

We use First Conditional to talk about future possibilities:
If we keep using cars, air pollution **will get** worse.
There **will be** shortages **if we continue** to waste water.

3 Read the magazine article again and complete the sentences.

1. If more people pick up after their dogs, _____.
2. What will happen _____?
3. _____, we will soon forget what a starry sky is!
4. _____, will I use less water than if I take a bath?
5. If we share our cars, _____.

4 🎧¹³ Listen to the interview and mark (✓) the topics that the people talk about.

washing the dishes ☐   plastic waste ☐   consuming energy ☐
washing clothes ☐   recycling waste ☐   using electricity at home ☐

5 🎧¹³ Listen again and mark T (True) or F (False).

1. If we use compact fluorescent bulbs instead of regular lightbulbs, we will save 25% more energy.   T F
2. Washing dishes by hand uses less water than a dishwasher.   T F
3. Using cold water in a washing machine is not as good for washing clothes as using hot water.   T F
4. The biggest user of energy at home is electrical equipment.   T F
5. Every time we leave the refrigerator door open, we waste energy.   T F

6 Think Fast! Read the conditions and consequences. Then connect the sentences using the first conditional.

5 min

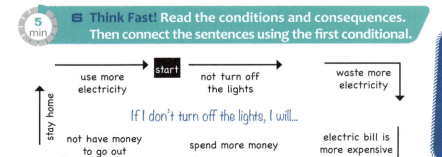

Guess What!

In the United States, it takes 25 large power stations to provide electricity for all the refrigerators in the country for one year.

Reading and Writing

1 Look and write the headings.

- Being Vegetarian
- Wearing Fur Coats
- Keeping Animals in Zoos

I'm not against wearing animal fur. We use **leather** for shoes, belts and jackets—so why shouldn't we use fur for coats and hats? ☐

I don't agree with killing animals for their fur. It's wrong and it's **cruel**. There are many alternatives that are **stylish** and warm. ☐

Zoos are good for the environment. They help to conserve animals that are in danger in the wild. And they're a great way for kids to learn about wild animals. ☐

I'm against having zoos. Animals are **confined** in small areas so they can't move freely. Besides, they are fed by humans, so they can't hunt for food. They will never be able to live in the wild again. ☐

There are many reasons to be vegetarian. Firstly, meat isn't good for our bodies. Secondly, it isn't right to kill animals for food. And finally, it requires a lot of water and land to keep animals. Growing **crops** is much less **wasteful**. ☐

There's nothing wrong with eating meat. Humans are omnivores, and meat does have a lot of protein. Plus, it tastes really good! ☐

2 Read the statements. Write *F* (For) or *A* (Against).

3 Read the statements on page 46 again. Which arguments do you agree with? Underline the arguments that sound more convincing.

4 Complete the opinion expressions.
   1. There are _____ to be vegetarian.
   2. There's _____ with eating meat.
   3. Zoos are _____ the environment.
   4. I'm _____ having zoos.
   5. I'm _____ wearing animal fur.
   6. I _____ with killing animals for their fur.

5 Choose a topic from page 46. Write a sentence to state your opinion using an expression from Activity 4.
   _____

6 Add two or three reasons to support your opinion.
   _____
   _____
   _____

Be Strategic!
Be more persuasive. State your opinion in a clear way and give reasons to support your opinion.

Stop and Think! How can you develop an informed opinion about something?

Glossary
leather: a material made from animal skin
cruel: causing pain and suffering
stylish: in style; fashionable
confined: locked in an area
crops: plants that are used for food
wasteful: using resources in an inefficient way

Culture

1 **Read and number the photos.**

1. In Japan, many businesses have *Maneki neko* cat figures for good luck!
2. The people of Okinawa, in southern Japan, have very distinct food. One dish is *umi budo*—a type of **seaweed** that tastes like **caviar**.
3. Sumo wrestling is a popular sport in Japan. Good sumo wrestlers should be very heavy. They **skip** breakfast and sleep after meals to help them gain weight!
4. In the spring, white and pink cherry **blossoms** appear all over Japan. People have picnics and parties in parks to enjoy them. There are even cherry-blossom flavored snacks.

2 Read the article. Is nuclear energy a good option? Why or why not?

Nuclear Energy in Japan

Japan is home to 127 million people, and is about the size of the State of California. Japan doesn't have a lot of fossil fuels, so it needs to buy them from other countries to generate electricity. They also have more than 50 nuclear reactors, which can generate energy without carbon emissions. But now they're only using a few of these reactors. What happened?

In 2011, there was a large earthquake near the coast of Japan. It was very powerful, measuring 9.0 on the Richter scale. It caused a tsunami that damaged some nuclear reactors at the Fukushima power plant. The damaged reactors emit *radiation*, energy particles that can make people very sick. Everyone who lived near the power plant was **evacuated**—nearly 450,000 people—and even after several years, more than 100,000 people can't return to their homes. In addition, the power plant continues to **leak radioactive** water, which is collected so that it doesn't flow into the ocean. It leaks several tons of contaminated water every day. Now a plan is in place to reduce the flow of water, but it will take 30 to 40 years to clean up the site.

For this reason, people in Japan don't see nuclear energy as a safe option. They plan to close the last few nuclear power plants. Now they have an opportunity to use and develop new forms of clean energy.

3 🎧¹⁴ Listen and answer. Why is the town of Kamikatsu a special place?

4 🎧¹⁴ Listen again and circle T (True) or F (False).

1. Kamikatsu is a small town in northern Japan.   T   F
2. The population of Kamikatsu is about 2,000.   T   F
3. They don't have a garbage truck.   T   F
4. They wash their garbage.   T   F
5. There are 20 recycling categories.   T   F
6. They make new things using old clothes.   T   F

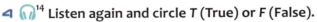

Stop and Think! How can you create less garbage?

Glossary
seaweed: an ocean plant
caviar: fish eggs
skip: to not do something
blossoms: flowers
evacuated: moved to a safe place
leak: to lose liquid from a container
radioactive: contaminated with radiation

Project

1 Look and match the symbols with the slogans.

2 🎧¹⁵ Listen to the scripts and mark (✓) the topics.

3 🎧¹⁵ Number the missing fragments of each script. Then listen again and check.

1. Be cool. Don't **litter**.   2. garbage trucks don't collect   3. in bottles, bags
4. reduce, reuse and recycle   5. throw **trash** out of their cars   6. will have less trash
7. will ever visit our area   8. sort our trash

Script 1	In general, people in our community care about the environment. We ____ and take paper, plastic, glass and metal to the special **dumpster** to recycle. The problem is that the dumpster is always full because the ____ recycling every day. I really think they should, so that people don't have to leave the trash around the dumpster. It is also important to reduce the number of containers we use. If we reuse containers, we ____. So remember: ____!
Script 2	A growing problem in our neighborhood is littering. Some people ____ or leave it in the park, on the grass. In some places, the ground is covered ____ and **wrappers**. It's **infuriating**! If people continue littering like this, no one ____, we will harm the wildlife and pollute the environment. We should work together, clean up the mess and live in a healthy and beautiful place. It is time to say: ____!

Guess What!
You don't need to be an important political figure to change your community. There are thousands—maybe millions—of teen activists in the world. They see a problem and look for a way to solve it.

Glossary
litter: throw garbage in public places
trash: garbage
dumpster: a large container for trash
wrappers: covers for food items
infuriating: making someone very angry

◀ **Make a mini documentary about your community.**

1. Work with a group. Discuss different activities that help or hurt the environment in your community.
2. Choose one or more activities to feature in your mini documentary.
3. Write a script similar to the one in Activity 3 for your video. Explain why an action has a positive or negative impact.
4. Make a three minute video to present your information. Use images from the community to demonstrate the activities.

Review

1 **Read and complete the sentences.**

> conserve   emissions   energy   fossil   landfills   planting   pollute   saves

1. Many cars and buses use _____ fuels.
2. Turn off the lights when you leave a room. It _____ electricity.
3. Reuse and recycle. Send less garbage to _____.
4. _____ water! It's a precious resource.
5. You can improve your neighborhood by _____ trees.
6. Traditional power plants _____ the environment.
7. Use clean _____ like solar and wind energy.
8. Buying local products is a good way to reduce your carbon _____.

2 **Look and label the actions.**

1. c_____ w_____
2. s_____ e_____
3. p_____ the e_____
4. r_____ c_____ e_____
5. s_____ g_____ to l_____
6. p_____ t_____
7. u_____ c_____ e_____
8. u_____ f_____ f_____

3 Read and circle the correct option.

Is it too late to save the planet?

The climate is changing. The arctic is warming. Some cities have air pollution that makes people sick. Is it too late to save the planet? I don't think so. If we (1) **make / will** make changes now, we (2) **make / can make** a difference. With new technologies, we can reduce our carbon footprint to zero. It's easy to think only countries and companies can change things, but small decisions are important, too. We (3) **have / will have** a lot less garbage if we (4) **start / will start** reusing and recycling more. And if we (5) **choose / will choose** earth-friendly products—without toxic chemicals or a large carbon footprint—companies (6) **make / will make** more earth-friendly products. If everyone (7) **cares / will care** about the environment, the situation (8) **improve / will improve**. Make a change today!

4 Unscramble the questions.

1. what / on / the / will / we / throw / happen / if / trash / ground / ?
   _____
   The city will look dirty.

2. happen / what / if / the / we / pollute / will / air / ?
   _____
   People will get sick.

3. pollute / what / happen / we / the / will / if / oceans / ?
   _____
   Fish and animals will die.

4. recycle / will / happen / what / we / if / ?
   _____
   We'll send less garbage to landfills.

5. we / clean / happen / will / what / use / energy / if / ?
   _____
   We'll have clean air and water.

Just for Fun

1 Read and complete the sentences.

> it will produce oxygen and clean the air
> you will keep them out of landfills
> you won't need any electricity or use any fossil fuels
> you can reduce your carbon footprint by 500%
> you will save up to 500 liters per month

Conserve Water
If you turn off the water when you wash your hair, _____!

Stop Sending Garbage to Landfills
Buy a cloth bag and use it when you shop. If you stop using plastic bags, _____—and prevent them from polluting the environment.

Reduce Carbon Emissions
If you eat chicken instead of beef, _____!

Save Electricity
You don't need to buy solar panels to use clean energy. If you use natural sunlight instead of a lamp, _____!

Plant Something… Anything!
Planting trees helps the environment, but all plants do! If you keep a small plant in your house, _____.

2 Look and classify the recyclable materials (1=plastic, 2=paper, 3=glass).

water bottles ☐

lightbulbs ☐

newspapers ☐

jars ☐

shampoo bottles ☐

cardboard boxes ☐

soda bottles ☐

toilet paper rolls ☐

Vocabulary

1 Look and underline the topic.

a. school activities   b. being a fan   c. house chores

2 🎧16 Listen and number the expressions.

☐ stand in line
☐ be good at
☐ wear a hat
☐ be a fan of
☐ put on face paint
☐ put up posters
☐ collect action figures
☐ dress up as characters
☐ get an autograph
☐ wear team colors

3 🎧16 Read and complete the speech bubbles. Then listen again and check.

| collect   colors   face   fan   get   good   hat   in   up (2x) |

MY PASSION IS FOOTBALL! I CAN'T WAIT FOR THE FALL WHEN FOOTBALL SEASON STARTS! IT'S FUN TO WEAR TEAM _____ ON GAME DAY. THEY'RE GREEN AND YELLOW. I PUT ON _____ PAINT, TOO. IT'S MESSY, BUT LOTS OF FUN. AND I WEAR A SILLY _____ FOR GOOD LUCK.

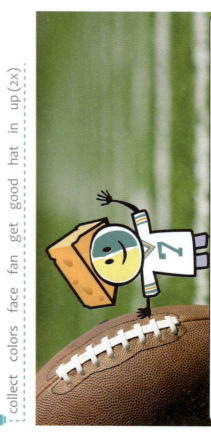

I AM A HUGE _____ OF ZOMBIES. I PUT _____ ZOMBIE POSTERS ALL OVER MY ROOM. MY FRIENDS AND I DRESS _____ AS MOVIE CHARACTERS. I'M REALLY _____ AT MOVIE MAKEUP, WITH **FAKE BLOOD** AND EVERYTHING.

56

4 Read and match.

1. stand in — colors
2. be good — at
3. get an — as characters
4. dress up — fan of
5. be a — hat
6. wear team — autograph
7. collect — line
8. put on — face paint
9. wear a — posters
10. put up — action figures

I AM A TOTAL STAR WARS **GEEK**. I HAVE ALL OF THE MAIN CHARACTERS. I TRY TO GET ACTION FIGURES AUTOGRAPHS AT CONVENTIONS. I HAVE DARTH VADER'S **SIGNATURE**! I HAD TO STAND IN LINE FOR THREE HOURS TO GET IT!

5 Read and complete the sentences.

1. Our _____ are blue and orange.
2. I'll _____ all day to get a concert ticket.
3. You're really _____ playing the saxophone.
4. I _____ soccer **jerseys**. I have eight of them!
5. My brothers always go to conventions to get _____.
6. My friends and I _____ face paint to every game.
7. We need to _____ as dragons for the party.
8. Are you a _____ of superhero movies?

6 Describe the picture using the expressions from Activity 4.

_____
_____
_____
_____
_____

7 Think Fast! Write the fan activities in alphabetical order. Which activities do you do?

Guess What!
Did you ever miss a character at the end of a book or movie? *Fanfiction* is a writing genre where people write stories about characters. They often imagine new adventures or invent alternate endings.

Glossary
fake: not real
blood: red fluid in the body
geek: a fan of something unusual
signature: a person's name in cursive
jersey: a shirt used in team sports as part of a uniform

57

1 🎧17 Read the flyer. Then listen and write C (Carrie) or A (Andrea).

1. She's going to dress up as Katniss Everdeen. _____
2. She's going to dress up as Effie Trinket. _____

2 🎧17 Listen again and complete the phrases using intensifiers. What is the role of intensifiers?

1. really _____
2. a bit _____
3. pretty _____
4. extremely _____
5. so _____

Intensifiers	
extremely	→ !!!!
so	→ !!!
really	→ !!!
pretty	→ !!
a bit	→ !

3 Read and complete the dialogue.

Will: Hey, Lauren.
Lauren: Hi, Will.
Will: Did you see the new Star Trek movie?
Lauren: Yeah. It was (1) _____ (!!) cool. The special effects were (2) _____ (!!!) amazing.
Brian: Hi, Will! Hi, Lauren!
Lauren: Hi, Brian! What did you think about the Star Trek movie?
Brian: It was spectacular!—I mean (3) _____ (!!!!) entertaining. I'm seeing it again tomorrow night.
Will: Can I come along?
Brian: Sure! Coliseum Cinema?
Will: That's (4) _____ (!) far for me. Can we go somewhere closer?
Brian: No problem. Are you coming, too, Lauren?
Lauren: Sorry, guys. I have a big soccer match. But have fun!

Already, Yet

We use *yet* in questions and negative sentences:
Did you play any games yet?
I didn't play any games yet.

We use *already* for affirmative sentences:
I already played three games.

4 🎧 ¹⁸ **Listen and mark (✓) the correct option.**

1. Jo is dressed up as _____   ☐ a dragon.   ☐ an **alien**.
2. Elsie _____ wearing a costume.   ☐ is   ☐ isn't
3. Elsie _____ for the **contest** yet.   ☐ signed up   ☐ didn't sign up
4. Jo _____ signed up for the contest.   ☐ already   ☐ yet

5 Look at the map and write the sentences using *already* or *yet*.

1. Jo and Elsie / play / some games
   _____

2. they / not have / any snacks
   _____

3. they / not watch / a movie
   _____

4. they / see / the fan art exhibition
   _____

5. they / go / to the costume contest
   _____

 6 Think Fast! Imagine you are at the Sci-Fi Festival. Ask and answer five questions about the event.

Glossary
alien: an extraterrestrial life form
contest: a competition

Reading & Speaking

1 Read the descriptions. Which text describes a good listener?

1 It's not always cool to be friends with your mom, but my mom is the best. When I want to talk to her, she stops what she's doing and pays attention to me. She asks me things. I'm glad we're **close**.

2 My friend and I hang out a lot, but she's always looking at her phone. I'm never sure that she cares about what I'm saying. We have fun, though.

3 My brother and I never get along. The minute I say anything, he **interrupts** me. Or if I need to ask him something, he doesn't pay attention. He always asks, "Huh?" or "What?" instead of listening the first time!

Text _____ describes a good listener.

Be Strategic!
Active listening is an important communication—and speaking—skill. To be an active listener, concentrate on the other person's message. Be prepared to ask questions to check your understanding and to show interest.

2 Read the conversation and underline the questions.

Lily: My name is Lily and this is my new friend Renée. We're practicing active listening for our English class. What's your favorite activity, Renée? What are you passionate about?

Renée: That's pretty easy—cheerleading. I've **been** a cheerleader since I was five years old.

Lily: What do you do, I mean, as a cheerleader?

Renée: Well, we do cheers—like **chants**—and gymnastics at football and basketball games. And we go to cheerleading competitions, too.

Lily: What's that like?

Renée: It's a lot like a gymnastics or dance competition. We learn a routine and perform it in front of **judges**. We use pop songs for our routines. It's a lot of fun.

Lily: Is cheerleading a sport? I never thought of it that way before.

Renée: It is! And cheerleaders are athletes. We lift weights and exercise a lot.

Lily: How often do you **work out**?

Renée: I go to the gym almost every day.

Lily: I'm really impressed. When is your next competition? Maybe I can come and **cheer you on**!

Renée: It's this Saturday! Sure! Come and see us!

Glossary
close: with a good relationship

interrupt: to speak when someone else is speaking

been: the past participle of the verb *be*

chants: phrases repeated with a rhythm

judges: officials who give a score to a performer

work out: to exercise

cheer you on: to encourage someone to do something

3 **Complete and match.**

1. What _____ you do?
2. What's that _____?
3. _____ cheerleading a sport?
4. How _____ do you work out?
5. _____ is your next competition?

It's this Saturday.
It is!
It's a lot like gymnastics…
We do cheers…
I go to the gym almost every day.

4 🎧¹⁹ **Read the dialogue and complete the questions. Then listen and check.**

do   how   what   when   where

Patrick: So _____ is your passion, Damian?

Damian: My passion is train spotting. I'm a total train geek. I love trains, and I learn everything about very specific **engines**. Then I go places to take pictures of them.

Patrick: I don't know very much about train spotting. Aren't all trains the same? _____ are they different?

Damian: Each engine is kind of unique. It has different colors and logos, according to the company it belongs to. And they have different numbers on them. They even have different **horns**.

Patrick: _____ did you get interested in trains?

Damian: When I was little.

Patrick: And _____ do you go to see the trains?

Damian: I go to many places, but my favorite place is by the river. It's a really great place for pictures.

Patrick: _____ you have a favorite picture?

Damian: Yes. It's this one. A Union Pacific engine.

Patrick: That's pretty cool. Hey, thanks for sharing about your hobby.

Damian: You're welcome.

5 **Think Fast!** Choose a dialogue to read aloud with a classmate. Can you do it without making any mistakes?

6 What are you passionate about? Ask and answer with a classmate.

Stop and Think! What activities do you dislike? Is it ever good to do activities that are boring or unpleasant?

Glossary

engine: the part of a train with a motor, usually at the front of the train

horns: a part of a vehicle that makes a loud noise as a warning

Culture

1 Look at the map. Do you know what country it is?

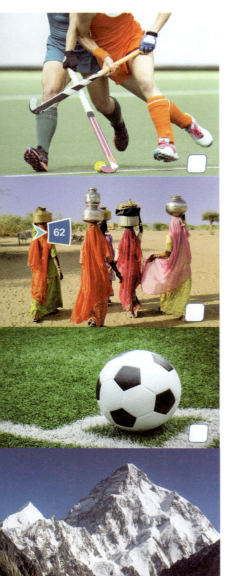

2 Read and number.

1. Pakistan is a country in South Asia. It borders four different countries: India, Afghanistan, Iran and China. In Pakistan, the main languages are English, Urdu, and Punjabi.

2. The largest city in Pakistan is Karachi, but the capital is Islamabad. *Abad* means city in Urdu.

3. K-2, the world's second highest peak, is located in Pakistan.

4. *Roh* is a popular drink in Pakistan. It's made of sugarcane juice and spices.

5. Cricket is the most popular sport in Pakistan, but field hockey is the national sport. Baseball is pretty popular there, too.

6. The Thar desert is located on the border between Pakistan and India. It's the world's ninth largest sub-tropical desert.

7. Pakistan makes more than 50% of the world's soccer balls and is a big producer of cotton.

8. Malala Yousafzai is a Pakistani activist. She believes strongly in education, especially for girls. In 2014, at the age of 17, she received the Nobel Peace Prize.

3 🎧²⁰ Listen and complete the table.

	Cricket	Street Cricket
History	the 18th century	the 19_____s
Teams	_____ players	_____ players
Equipment	a bat, a leather ball, helmets, pads and gloves	a _____ ball and a _____
Played	on a cricket pitch	in the _____

4 Read the article and write the headlines.

- Sports
- Agriculture in Pakistan
- Other Attractions
- An Annual Event

_____

Agriculture is a major industry in Pakistan. Seventy percent of the population works in this industry. The most important crops are **wheat**, sugarcane, cotton and rice. Pakistan is also the world's largest producer of mangoes. Livestock like cows, sheep, buffalo and goats are also important.

_____

In March of 2015, the Pakistani city of Lahore hosted the National Horse and Cattle Show. It took place in Fortress Stadium and lasted for several days. The show is a local tradition with a long history. It features exciting sports and entertaining shows.

_____

The Horse and Cattle Show is famous for equestrian sports: horse racing, polo and a local sport called _tent pegging_. Tent pegging is an ancient sport where the participant must hit a small **target** with a sword or a **lance**.

_____

There are many things to see at the National Horse and Cattle Show. People do **stunts** on motorcycles. There are **skydivers**. You can watch a military parade or dog races. There are dog shows and cattle shows, where participants compete to have the best animal. There are even events with dancing horses and camels. At night, there are fireworks and performances with **torches**.

5 Find and write the word.

1. the nationality of a person, place or thing in Pakistan _____
2. three cities in Pakistan _____
3. the national sport _____
4. a famous activist from Pakistan _____
5. an important industry _____
6. a common fruit in Pakistan _____
7. the season of the horse and cattle show _____
8. in tent pegging, a person rides this animal _____

 Stop and Think! How are farmers important to a community?

Glossary

wheat: a plant seed used to make bread

target: the object of attention or attack

lance: a long, sharp pole

stunts: tricks

skydivers: people who jump from a plane with parachutes

torches: sticks to carry fire from one place to another

Project

BOSTON
MASSACHUSSETTS
TOP 10 FUN FAN ACTIVITIES

ARE YOU A SPORTS FAN?

- Come and see the New England Patriots at Gillette Stadium! Their team colors are red, white, silver and blue.

- Visit historic Fenway Park and see the Red Sox play! It's a Boston pastime!

- Are you into basketball? Don't miss the Boston Celtics at TD Garden!

- The Boston Bruins are six-time Stanley Cup champions!

1 Look at the Fan Activities brochure. Who is this brochure for?

- sports fans ☐
- music fans ☐
- international food fans ☐
- history fans ☐
- science fans ☐
- art and literature fans ☐

2 Read the brochure and circle the correct option.

1. These are activities you can do in **Atlanta** / **Boston** / **Chicago**.
2. The Red Sox are a **basketball** / **baseball** / **hockey** team.
3. The Stanley Cup is a **football** / **basketball** / **hockey** trophy.
4. Visits to the **science museum** / **aquarium** / **observatory** are free in the evenings.
5. *Doro wot* is an **Irish** / **Ethiopian** / **Italian** dish.

ARE YOU A SCIENCE FAN?

- The Museum of Science is an excellent destination! Learn about dinosaurs, butterflies, clean energy and space travel.

- Come to see the New England Aquarium! They have penguins, sea turtles and marine animals. You can even go on a whale watch!

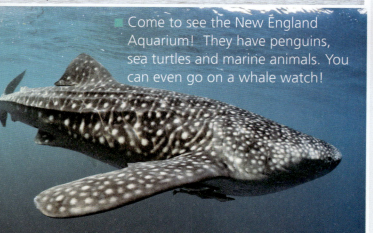

- Are you an astronomy fan? Boston has seven different observatories. Night time admission is free!

ARE YOU A FAN OF INTERNATIONAL CUISINE?

- Irish heritage is important in Boston, and there are dozens of Irish restaurants to try. Shepherd's pie is a classic dish!

- Ethiopian food is also popular in Boston. Doro wot (chicken in sauce) is a popular dish, but be careful! It can be very spicy!

- Every American city has Mexican restaurants, but Boston has restaurants from many Latin American countries! Try Chilean or Peruvian food today!

▲ Tacos

- Boston offers European cuisines, too: enjoy dishes from Spain, Italy, Poland, Germany or Greece! Mmm!

▲ Polish Pierogi

3 Choose a city or region and complete the mind map. What kinds of fans are happy there? What activities can they do?

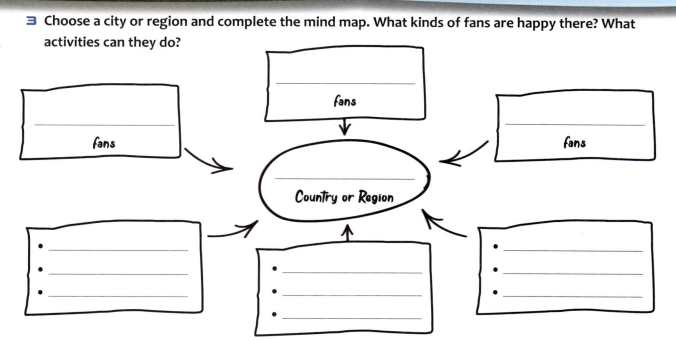

4 Make a Fan Activities brochure and present it to the class.

Review

1 Complete the questions. Then read and match.

1. Do you collect _____ figures?
2. What are you _____ at?
3. Did you ever _____ an autograph from someone?
4. How long would you _____ in line for something?
5. What are you a _____ of?
6. Do you ever _____ up as a character?

I'm a fan of cooking competitions. I love watching them!

Yes! I collect DC Comics figures. Mostly the Green Lantern.

Maybe for half an hour. I'm not a very patient person.

Only on Halloween! Last year, I went as Kylo Ren from Star Wars.

When I was little, a famous basketball player signed my T-shirt.

I'm good at drawing. I do a lot of manga.

2 Look and write a fan activity.

1 _____

2  _____

3  _____

4  _____

3 Read and underline the intensifiers. Write them on the lines.

I have many interests, but I'm a big fan of *Doctor Who*. It's an extremely popular sci-fi TV show from the UK. It's about a guy who has special powers—the Doctor. He can travel through time and space in a TARDIS. It looks like a blue police box, but it's really big inside. He fights against the Daleks. They're part alien, part robot, and they want to "exterminate" everyone. It's a lot of fun to watch *Doctor Who*. When I first saw the show, I thought it was a bit silly, but now I think it's so awesome. Even my friends think it's pretty cool.

1. _____ 3. _____
2. _____ 4. _____ 5. _____

4 Look and write !, !!, !!! or !!!! next to the intensifiers.

5 Read and describe using intensifiers. Choose and circle the adjective.

1. your town or city   It's _____ big / small.
2. your favorite movie   It's _____ exciting / romantic.
3. kids' movies   They're _____ fun / silly.
4. typical American food   It's _____ good / bad.

6 Write sentences using the cues and *already* or *yet*.

1. we / see the fan art exhibition → +

_____

2. Sam / get the concert tickets → -

_____

3. Allison / watch the new movie → ?

_____

4. you / complete your costume → ?

_____

5. they / read the book → -

_____

Just for Fun

1 Read and mark (✓) the friends' interests.

Kylie, Olivia, Will, Jake and Max have many interests, but they're all different. Can you guess who likes what?

 Kylie isn't interested in sports. She doesn't go to games or have any favorite athletes. She does like to collect things, though. She's always buying new action figures.

Olivia likes sports a lot, and she goes to all of the games at her school. She supports her team at every game.

 Will is also interested in sports. He goes to games all over the world, and has a big collection of autographed hats, balls and T-shirts.

Jake is a movie fan. He memorizes lines and facts about the actors. He has movie posters all over his room.

 Max isn't a sports fan or a movie fan. He likes wearing costumes, and when he isn't dressed up, he's at home playing video games.

	collects athletes' autographs	dresses up as video game characters	collects action figures	is a fan of a team	collects movie posters
Kylie					
Olivia					
Will					
Jake					
Max					

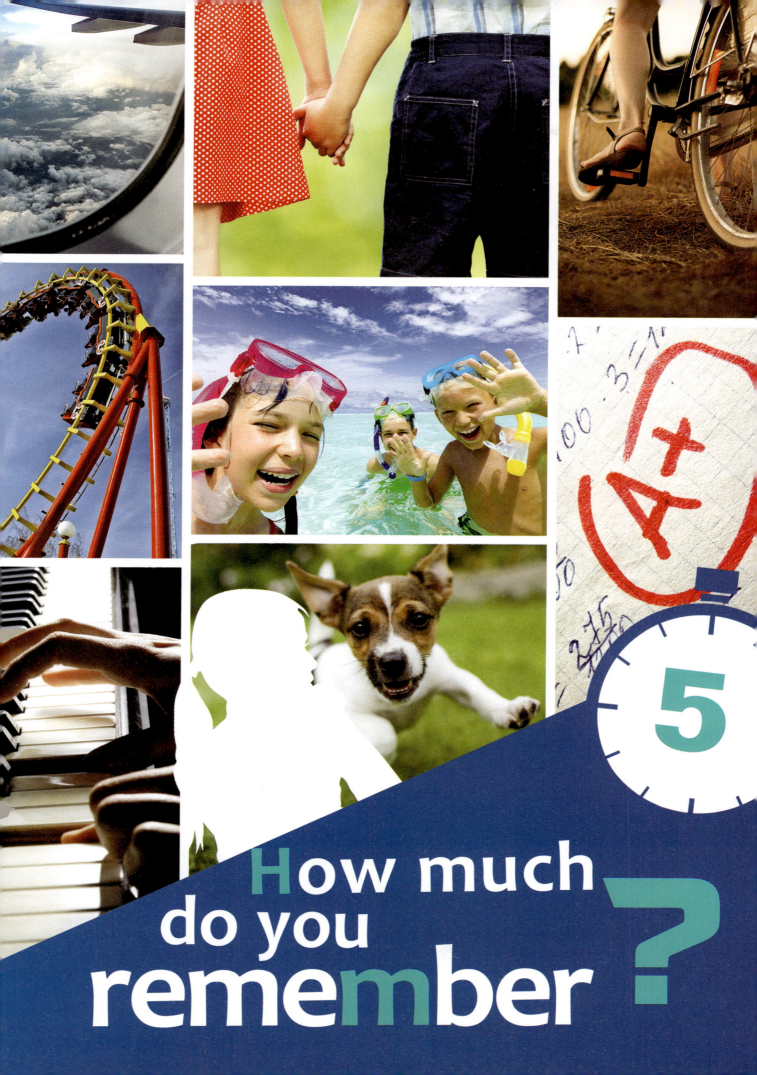

1 Look and number the pictures.

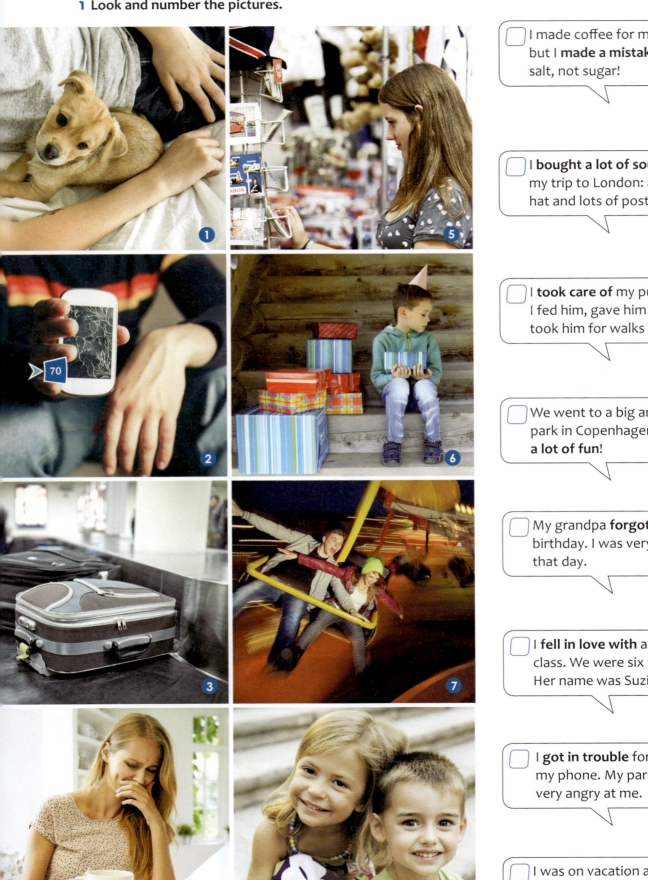

- I made coffee for my mom, but I **made a mistake**. I added salt, not sugar!
- I **bought a lot of souvenirs** on my trip to London: a T-shirt, a hat and lots of postcards.
- I **took care of** my puppy, Zak. I fed him, gave him water, and took him for walks every day.
- We went to a big amusement park in Copenhagen. We **had a lot of fun**!
- My grandpa **forgot** my birthday. I was very sad that day.
- I **fell in love with** a girl in my class. We were six years old. Her name was Suzie.
- I **got in trouble** for breaking my phone. My parents were very angry at me.
- I was on vacation and my suitcase **got lost**. The airline put it on a different plane.

2 Read and circle the correct option.
1. I **took care of / forgot** my baby brother while my mom was working.
2. I **made a mistake / had a lot of fun** and dialed a wrong number.
3. She **got in trouble / got lost** for arriving home late.
4. I **forgot / bought** a present for my friend and she loved it.
5. He **fell in love with / got lost** his dad's new car.

3 🎧²¹ Listen and match the people with the keepsakes.

seashell   toy car   necklace   drawing   baby tooth

Guess What!
Photos and *keepsakes*—objects from important events—are common ways to remember the past. But music, smells and flavors can also help you remember information and experiences.

4 Read the description. Then write the name of the keepsake.
1. It's shiny. It's metal with tiny white crystals. Maybe they're diamonds. _____
2. It is red. One of the wheels is broken. _____
3. It's smooth and shiny. It's pink on the inside and white and brown on the outside. _____
4. It's small and white. It's not really shiny. _____
5. It's in an old notebook. It's a dinosaur with big teeth. _____

5 Think Fast! Classify the keepsakes.

something that you make	something you wear	something you play with	something that falls out	something you find in nature

1 Look and number the scenes.

Past Continuous

We use Past Continuous to describe actions that happen for a period of time in the past:
The children **were playing** all day.
My computer **wasn't working** yesterday.

2 🎧²² **Listen and underline the cause of the problem.**

a. The weather was bad.
b. One of the swimmers got tired.
c. The currents were strong.

3 🎧²² **Listen again and and circle T (True) or F (False).**

	T	F
1. A family was relaxing at the beach.	T	F
2. A man and kids weren't having fun in the sea.	T	F
3. Some tourists saw the family and **raised the alarm**.	T	F
4. Some **lifeguards** were teaching a course nearby.	T	F
5. A man was crying.	T	F

4 Think Fast! Find and underline the verbs in the past continuous in Activity 3.

Glossary

exhausted: very tired
raise the alarm: to call for help
lifeguards: expert swimmers trained to rescue swimmers at pools and beaches
lucky: fortunate

Past Continuous and Past Simple: When

Past Continuous + when + Past Simple → a continuous action that is interrupted:
The family **was swimming** when strong currents **pulled** them away from the beach.

Past Continuous   Past Simple

5 Match the parts of the sentences.

1. Three members of a family were swimming (...)   —   when they heard the dad shouting for help.

2. Other family members were relaxing at the beach   —   the children were crying.

3. Lifeguards were teaching a first-aid course   —   when they got into trouble.

4. When we located the family,   —   when they realized there was a problem and raised the alarm.

6 Read the excerpts and write the headings.

 An Earthquake   A Tornado    A Flood

_____

It was a typical morning in Hudson, Ohio. (1) <u>Most people were driving to work while others were shopping or going to school.</u> (2) <u>While the crew at the local fire station were cleaning the fire engines, Chief Brown was having his morning coffee.</u> (3) <u>He was checking his e-mail when he heard the phone.</u> He answered and dropped his coffee on the floor. They had a real problem and it was coming in their direction at 100 kilometers per hour…

_____

Sarah was on vacation in Acapulco with her parents and a dog. One day at the beach, (4) <u>Sarah was playing with the dog while her parents were swimming in the sea.</u> (5) <u>She was just throwing a ball when she felt the earth moving under her feet.</u> She turned around and saw the lifeguards shouting for people to evacuate the beaches. The palm trees started to move from side to side…

_____

(6) <u>David was looking out the window at the river while his mother was preparing breakfast.</u> (7) <u>He was thinking about the heavy rain when he saw that the water level in the river was going up quickly.</u> (8) <u>He was getting ready to tell his mom about it when someone knocked hard on their front door.</u> He realized something was very wrong…

Guess What!
When we talk about two simultaneous actions in the past, we use *while*:
I **was reading** a book while my dad **was watching** TV.

Past Continuous
Past Continuous

7 Read the underlined sentences in Activity 6. Then write S (Simultaneous) or I (Interrupted).

1. ___ 2. ___ 3. ___ 4. ___ 5. ___ 6. ___ 7. ___ 8. ___

Reading & Listening

1 Look and mark (✓) the topic of the article.

☐ the parts of the brain and memory   ☐ the organs of the body   ☐ the brain

How do you remember?

The brain is an organ that works like a very powerful computer. It doesn't have **wires** like a real computer, but it does have nerve cells, or *neurons*. Neurons transfer electricity and chemicals across the brain. One neuron can connect with many other neurons to create a *network*. When you learn something, new connections form between neurons. When you practice something—playing an instrument, doing ballet or using a foreign language—you make even more connections. More connections make it easier to do the activity again.

How do we make memories? A single memory can have many different types of information. Your brain processes the things you see, hear, smell, feel and think all at the same time. This information goes to a part of the brain called the *hippocampus*. The hippocampus is in the center of the brain, but it is connected to many other parts of the brain. After the hippocampus processes new memories, they go to the *cerebral cortex*. This is the "skin" of the brain. It isn't smooth like the outside of other organs. It has many folds, which helps it to **store** more information.

To remember information, the brain **replays** the pattern of electrical signals from the original event. This happens in many different parts of the brain so that you can remember what you saw, heard, smelled, felt and thought. Your brain is good at replaying memories in some situations. For example, you can easily remember the lyrics to your favorite song when it plays on the radio. The music you hear connects to similar information in your brain and helps you to remember the words. But if you try to remember the lyrics without the music, it's more difficult. For this reason, it can be difficult to remember facts for a test or a friend's phone number.

2 Read the article and label.

the cerebral cortex   the hippocampus   network   neuron

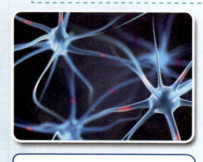

Be Strategic!
You can get a general idea of a text by looking at photos and diagrams, but to understand more deeply, look for the connections between images and specific parts of the text.

Glossary
wires: long, thin pieces of metal that conduct electricity

store: to keep; save

replay: to play something again

3 **Read again and complete the sentences.**
   1. Nerve _____ and neurons are the same things.
   2. Neurons transfer _____ and chemicals across the brain.
   3. New _____ form when you learn something.
   4. You get better at an activity when your _____ have more connections.
   5. Memories form in the _____ in the center of the brain.
   6. Then memories go to the _____ cortex.
   7. When you remember something, your brain _____ the pattern of electrical signals.

4 🎧²³ **Listen and circle the correct option.**

   1. It's easy to let **technology / computers** remember for you.
      - _____
      - _____

   2. Remembering keeps your brain active and **healthy / ready**.
      - _____

   3. The **first / next** strategy is to take care of yourself.
      - _____
      - _____
      - _____

   4. Write **things / notes** down.
      - _____

   5. **Give / Get** your brain a job.
      - _____

Guess What!
Mnemonic devices are strategies to help you remember specific information. For example, making a chant or song can help you to remember lists or names.

5 🎧²³ **Read and complete the notes in Activity 4. Then listen again and check.**

   manage stress   like a muscle   teach someone   information online
   enough sleep   your phone   healthy diet   pen or pencil

6 **Think Fast!** Choose one item and try to memorize the information. Can you remember it when time is up?
(3 min)

bananas   milk
bread   cheese
shampoo   eggs
cereal

2020 Market Street
San Francisco, CA

Welcome
the free encyclopedia that anyone can edit
5,141,465 articles in English

The largest cities in Germany are Berlin, Hamburg, Munich and Cologne.

Marie Jackson
📞 (412) 555-1026
✉ mj358@academy.net
🎂 November 9th

Culture

1 Read and complete the sentences.

Ayers Rock   3%   didgeridoo   kangaroo   forty-five thousand

1. Aboriginal Australians migrated to the country more than _____ years ago.
2. Aboriginal peoples constitute _____ of the Australian population.
3. _____ or *Uluru* is a sacred mountain for the Aboriginal Australians.
4. Aboriginal Australians are famous for the music played on a _____, a type of wooden instrument.
5. Many words for animals and places in Australia come from their languages, for example, _____, kookaburra and koala.

2 Read the article. Then write the underlined words under the correct images.

Aboriginal Australians

Aboriginal Australians have a **remarkable** and ancient culture. In fact, they have the oldest living cultural history in the world. They believe that humans, animals, plants and rocks date to a period called Dreamtime. This is when the spirits appeared and created humans, animals and the landscape as it is today. When they finished creating everything, the spirits changed into trees, stars, rocks, **watering holes** and humans. Aboriginals refer to the act of creation as *Dreaming*.

The myths related to Dreaming are called *songlines*. Songlines contain details about the landscape, so by singing them in the right sequence, it was possible for Aboriginals to navigate **vast** distances across the Australian outback and survive in difficult conditions.

the objective of leaving traces of their culture for future generations. Art has always been important to the Aboriginal Australians as a link between past and present, myths and reality. You can find examples of rock paintings on the sacred mountain of Uluru in the central Australian desert.

For the last thirty years, the world has been hearing more and more about the Aboriginal arts. Today's artists still create traditional designs, such as **dot** painting to produce beautiful outline figures, animals and natural features of the landscape. In 2007, Emily Kame Kngwarreye's piece *Earth's Creation* sold for over a million dollars.

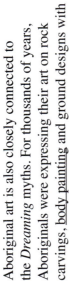

Aboriginal art is also closely connected to the *Dreaming* myths. For thousands of years, Aboriginals were expressing their art on rock carvings, body painting and ground designs with

3 Look at the pictures. Do you know what place it is?

a r G t e   r e B r a r i   e R f e

4 🎧24 Listen and unscramble the name of the place.

5 🎧24 Listen again and number the questions in order.

☐ Are there any threats to the GBR?
☐ Is it a Natural Wonder of the World?
☐ Where is the GBR located?
☐ Is it true that you can see it from outer space?

6 Match the questions with the answers.

1. Yes, it is. _____
2. It's off the coast of Australia. _____
3. 1,500 types. _____
4. It is 2,000 km long and 180 m high. _____
5. It's made of coral. _____
6. Yes! _____
7. The GBR faces several threats. _____

Stop and Think! Are there natural wonders under threat in your country?

☐ How big is it?
☐ How many types of fish live there?
☐ What is it made of?

Glossary

remarkable: extraordinary, special
watering hole: a place where you can find water
vast: very large
dot: a point

77

1 Look at the timeline on page 79 and choose the correct option.

1. What became available on October 23, 2001?
   a. iPod　　　　　　b. iPhone　　　　　c. iPad
2. Facebook was online _____ Youtube.
   a. before　　　　　b. after　　　　　　c. at the same time as
3. The 2012 Olympic Games opened in London on _____.
   a. June 18th　　　b. July 4th　　　　c. July 27th
4. Aaron has _____ brothers and sisters.
   a. no　　　　　　　b. two　　　　　　　c. three
5. His birthday is in _____.
   a. June　　　　　　b. April　　　　　　c. December

2 Classify the events from Aaron's timeline. Write *PE* or *WE*.

Barack Obama　　　　_____
move to Dallas　　　　_____
Emily　　　　　　　　_____
Harry Potter　　　　_____
Facebook　　　　　　_____
Aaron's birth　　　　　_____
iPod　　　　　　　　　_____
kindergarten　　　　　_____
baby Noah　　　　　　_____
Olympic Games　　　　_____
seventh grade　　　　_____
vacation in Spain　　　_____
tsunami　　　　　　　_____
YouTube　　　　　　　_____

Personal Experiences

World Events

3 List seven important personal events for you and your family. Write the dates.

Event	Date

◀ **Make a personalized timeline. Use Aaron's timeline as a model.**

My Personalized Timeline
by Aaron Taylor

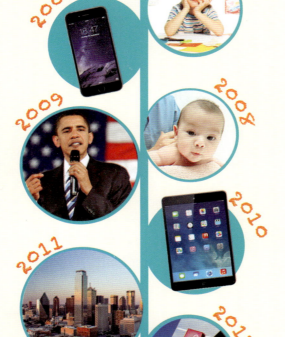

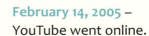

June 5, 2001 – I was born.

October 23, 2001 – Stores began selling first generation iPod.

November 4, 2001 – *Harry Potter and the Sorcerer's Stone* opened in movie theaters.

April 23, 2003 – My sister Emily was born.

February 4, 2004 – Mark Zuckerberg launched Facebook.

December 26, 2004 – The deadliest tsunami in history occured in the Indian Ocean.

February 14, 2005 – YouTube went online.

August 28, 2006 – I started kindergarten.

June 29, 2007 – The first iPhones went on the market.

December 1, 2008 – My brother Noah was born.

January 20, 2009 – Barack Obama became the first African American President of the United States.

January 27, 2010 – The first iPads became available.

May 2, 2011 – My family moved to Dallas, Texas.

July 7, 2011 – *Harry Potter and the Deathly Hollows, Part 2* opened in the UK.

July 27, 2012 – The 2012 Olympic Games opened in London.

September 3, 2013 – I started seventh grade in junior high school.

June 10, 2016 – I went on a trip to Barcelona, Spain.

Review

1 Unscramble names of keepsakes. Then read and number the questions.

1. kalecnec _____
2. ybtb ohota _____
3. yat roc _____
4. ingradw _____
5. hessaell _____

☐ What can you wear on your neck?
☐ What do you find at the beach?
☐ What falls out as a child grows older?
☐ What is a form of art?
☐ What can you play with?

2 Circle and correct the mistakes.

1. I take care in my little brother. _____
2. She buys much souvenirs when she travels. _____
3. I do a lot of math mistakes. _____
4. I fall in love of Emma Watson every time I see a photo of her. _____
5. We get in trouble with being rude to our teachers. _____

3 Write sentences using the past simple.

1. forget / her name / at the party
   I _____

2. buy / a T-shirt / at the stadium
   My sister _____

3. cell phone / get lost / during P.E. class
   His _____

4. have fun / with our friends / yesterday
   We _____

5. get in trouble / for / draw on the wall
   My brother _____

6. make several mistakes / in my German homework
   I _____

7. fall in love with / my new computer
   My friend _____

4 Read and complete the text message.

dancing
eating
having
listening
losing
playing
talking
watching

Jan online

Hi, we missed you at the party last night. You didn't miss much, it was really boring. I was with Lola the whole evening. I was (1) _____ to her problems. She gets in trouble with her teachers all the time! Ed and Frank were (2) _____ with the new girl from Denmark. She is very pretty, by the way. Elena and Lila were (3) _____ incredible amounts of pizza—they seemed really hungry! Greg was (4) _____ the football game on a big screen, but he wasn't (5) _____ a good time. His team was (6) _____. People weren't (7) _____ because Eva was only (8) _____ sad love songs. I think she is in love. Anyway, how are you?

☺ Type a message

5 Read and circle the correct option.

1. I was sleeping **while / when** the earthquake started.
2. She was dancing **while / when** he was watching football.
3. My sister was playing with the dog **while / when** I was doing homework.
4. My parents were driving home **while / when** they heard the news.
5. I was thinking about her **while / when** I remembered it was her birthday.

6 Complete the sentences using the correct forms of the verbs.

rain run see start try

1. It was _____ while I was walking to the bus stop and I didn't have an umbrella!
2. Later, I was standing at the bus stop when I _____ a man with an enormous dog.
3. I was looking at the dog in admiration when suddenly it _____ barking at me.
4. The dog was pulling the man towards me while he was _____ behind him.
5. I was _____ to decide what to do when I realized it was my uncle Mack and the puppy I took care of last year during the summer. The puppy recognized me!

Just for Fun

1. **In two minutes, find the following words in the unit and memorize the page number where each one appears. Then write the page numbers without looking.**

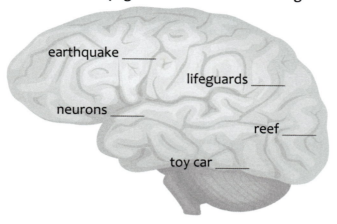

earthquake _____

lifeguards _____

neurons _____

reef _____

toy car _____

2. **In two minutes, scan the pages of the unit. Try to remember as many details as you can. Then answer the questions without looking.**

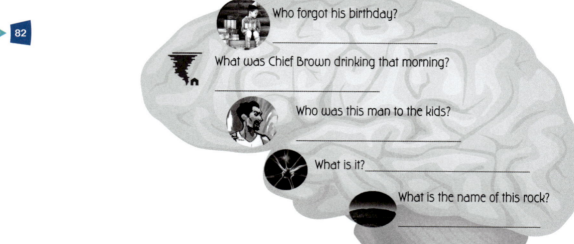

Who forgot his birthday? _____

What was Chief Brown drinking that morning? _____

Who was this man to the kids? _____

What is it? _____

What is the name of this rock? _____

3. **Read the story in pairs. Then follow the instructions to find out what happened.**

> A lifeguard walked into a restaurant in a small town on the coast. The waiter was talking to a customer when he saw the lifeguard. He went over and asked him what he wanted to eat. The lifeguard said something to him quietly and asked only for a glass of water. He was waiting for the water, looking at the sea when he heard a noise and jumped. (The waiter threw the glass of water on the floor next to him and it broke.) The lifeguard smiled, said thank you and left.

a. Choose Student A and Student B.
b. Student A – go to page 158 and read the answer. Remember it.
c. Student B – ask Student A *Yes / No* questions.
d. Student B – just answer *Yes* or *No*.

Examples of questions:
Was the lifeguard hungry?
Did the lifeguard know the waiter?
Was the lifeguard feeling well?

What do you need to travel?

6

Vocabulary

1 🎧²⁵ **Listen and mark (✓) the vacation destination.**

a busy restaurant   an airport   a ski resort   a water park   a mountain trail   a beach

2 🎧²⁶ **Listen and number the activities.**

The island of Santorini in Greece

 book a flight   exchange money

 get a passport   pack a suitcase

 stay in a hotel   hire a guide

 catch a train

3 Read the descriptions and write the travel activity.

1. I went to a government office. I took some papers and two small photos. They gave me a small book with my personal information in it. _____

2. We used a computer to look at different schedules and prices. We used a credit card to pay, and they sent us an e-mail with our **itinerary**. _____

3. Two or three days before my trip, I started collecting clothing and items in a large rectangular bag. I hope I didn't forget anything! _____

4. We had money in dollars, but we were visiting France. We went to a place at the airport, gave them dollars and got euros back. _____

5. We looked for a name of a person who knew a lot about the places we wanted to visit. All the special restaurants and attractions. And the history! _____

6. I went to a large building near the beach. It had a beautiful swimming pool. I took my things to a room with a bed and a TV. I stayed there for four days.
_____

7. Within France, we moved in a form of transportation that is slower than a plane, but you can see the landscape!
_____

Guess What!
The most popular tourist destination in the world is France with 84 million visitors a year. The United States is in second place with 75 million visitors.

4 Read and match.

Day 4 - Coyote Buttes, Utah

Today I hiked out to see "the wave" at Coyote Buttes. It's a beautiful rock formation in Utah. I got up at 5:30 to get ready: I packed plenty of water to drink—you get thirsty quickly in the desert—and a few snacks for when I get hungry. I put on comfortable clothes and hiking shoes. I wanted to get started before it got hot out, so I left the camp at 7:00. It took me six hours to get there because my **GPS** stopped working and I got lost. Fortunately, I found some other hikers who knew the way. Here's a photo of me looking at the site. It was amazing!

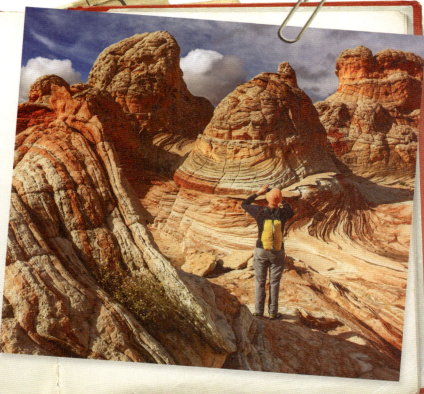

1. The Wave is — very early in the morning.
2. The hiker woke up — helped him find the destination.
3. To prepare, he — packed water and snacks.
4. The trip took six hours — because he got lost in the desert.
5. Some other hikers — a rock formation in Utah.

5 Read again and underline the expressions with *get*. Then complete the dictionary entries.

1. get _____ : to become hot
2. get _____ : to want to eat food
3. get _____ : to not know where you are
4. get _____ : to prepare for something
5. get _____ : to begin an activity
6. get _____ : to arrive
7. get _____ : to want to drink water
8. get _____ : to wake up

6 Think Fast! Write five sentences using *get*. (3 min)

1. _____
2. _____
3. _____
4. _____
5. _____

Glossary

reservation: an arrangement to use a business' services

itinerary: a travel schedule

GPS: a device that identifies your exact location

Grammar

1 Read and number the photos.

Study Abroad: Portugal!

Have you ever studied or lived in another country? Have you ever made friends from all over the world? The Jefferson International School has given this opportunity to thousands of students. It is located in the historic city of Lisbon, Portugal, and it offers a year abroad for high school students 16–18 years old.

The program includes:
1. the opportunity to learn Portuguese
2. **room and board** with a Portuguese **host family**
3. personal tutor support
4. a variety of competitive sports programs (sailing, surfing, tennis, soccer, swimming and basketball)
5. trips to cultural landmarks in Portugal and Spain

* Please note: All applicants must pass an entrance exam. For more information and applications contact: Eileen Powers, Admissions Officer epowers@jeffersoninternational.edu.pt

2 Complete the e-mail.

> heard a lot of   I am studying   program at Jefferson
> My cousin did a   send me   to Portugal before

To: Eileen Powers <epowers@jeffersoninternational.edu.pt>
Cc: Francesca Rossi <francesca.rossi15@email.com.it>
Subject: Application to Jefferson International School

Dear Ms. Powers,

I am interested in the study abroad (1) _____ International School. I'm Italian and am 16 years old. At the moment, (2) _____ at the Liceo Garibaldi in Milan. I haven't been (3) _____, but I have taken Portuguese lessons for a year.

I have (4) _____ good things about studying abroad. (5) _____ study abroad program recently, and she has had a wonderful experience.

Can you please (6) _____ an application for the program?

Sincerely,

Francesca Rossi

Present Perfect

We use *have* with past participles to talk about the present results of past actions:

She **has had** a wonderful experience.
I **haven't been** to Portugal.

Guess What!

We use the present perfect and *ever* to ask about life experiences: **Have** you **ever been** to England?

Glossary

room and board: a place to live and meals to eat

host family: a family that invites a person to stay in their home

scholarship: free tuition offered by a school or university

Present Perfect: Already, Yet

We use *already* with the present perfect for an event that has occurred:
He **has already made** some friends.
We use *yet* with questions and negative forms:
Have you **seen** anything interesting **yet**?
I haven't gone to any museums **yet**.

3 Write the past participles of the verbs. Use the ad and the e-mail on page 86.

1. study _____
2. live _____
3. make _____
4. give _____
5. be _____
6. take _____
7. hear _____
8. have _____

4 Complete the sentences using the present perfect.

1. I _____ (be) to Norway and Denmark.
2. She _____ (hear) about a program in Chile.
3. He _____ (live) with a host family before.
4. The school _____ (give) **scholarships** to fifteen international students.

5 **Think Fast!** In your notebook, write the past simple forms of the verbs in Activity 3. (5 min)

6 🎧²⁷ Listen and mark (✓) the correct option.

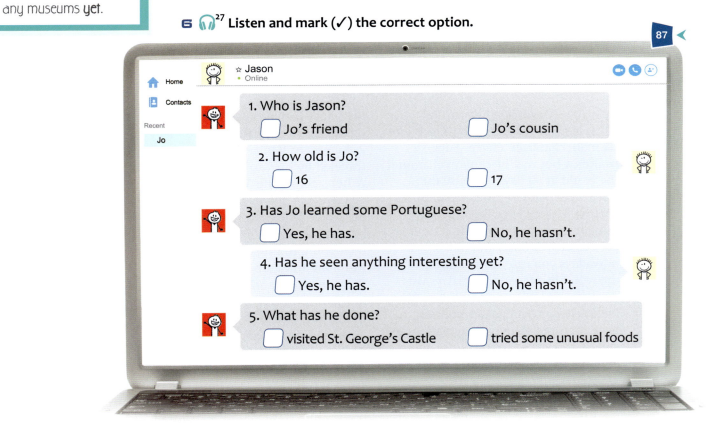

1. Who is Jason?
   ☐ Jo's friend   ☐ Jo's cousin
2. How old is Jo?
   ☐ 16   ☐ 17
3. Has Jo learned some Portuguese?
   ☐ Yes, he has.   ☐ No, he hasn't.
4. Has he seen anything interesting yet?
   ☐ Yes, he has.   ☐ No, he hasn't.
5. What has he done?
   ☐ visited St. George's Castle   ☐ tried some unusual foods

7 🎧²⁷ Listen again and complete using *already* or *yet*.

1. Have you learned Portuguese _____?
2. I've _____ learned a few expressions.
3. Have you made any friends _____?
4. Have you seen anything interesting _____?
5. I've _____ tried some unusual foods.

Reading & Listening

(Map with labels: London, England — DAY 1; _____, Italy; Mumbai, _____ — DAY 25; Alexandria, Egypt; Los Angeles, United States — DAY __; DAY 70; _____, United States)

Be Strategic!
Photos, maps and infographics can give clues to the type of information in a text and how it is organized.

1 Look at the map and mark (✓) the correct option.

1. This article probably lists…
   ☐ possible destinations for a future vacation.
   ☐ destinations in a trip around the world.
   ☐ modern forms of ocean transportation.

2. The information is probably organized…
   ☐ in chronological order.
   ☐ as a main point with supporting ideas.

2 Scan and complete the information on the map.

Around the World in 80 Days

¹ In Jules Verne's popular **novel** *Around the World in 80 Days*, the main character, Phileas Fogg, **makes a bet** that he can travel around the world in 80 days. Because the story takes place in the nineteenth century, Phileas Fogg can only travel using transportation from that time period, such as boats and trains. While nowadays you can travel around the world in a few days, 80 days was once an impressive accomplishment. Phileas Fogg's fictional adventures have captured readers' imaginations for almost 150 years, but this story doesn't end there.

² Michael Palin is a famous world traveler. He does travel programs for the BBC. His first program, also called *Around the World in 80 Days*, was based on Jules Verne's novel. Michael Palin traveled around the world in 80 days using Fogg's route and nineteenth-century forms of transportation.

³ Michael's **journey** started in London on a train **bound for** Italy. By Day 2, he was in Venice. From there he traveled by boat to Athens, and from Athens across the Mediterranean Sea. He reached Alexandria, Egypt on Day 7. In Egypt, he traveled by train and camel, and boarded a boat going to India. He arrived in Mumbai, India on Day 25. From there, he took a train and arrived in Madras on Day 29. He crossed the Indian Ocean by boat, arriving in Singapore on Day 38, Shanghai, China on Day 46 and Yokohama, Japan on Day 50. From there, he crossed the Pacific Ocean to Los Angeles. He arrived on Day 64. He traveled by train across the United States to get to New York on Day 70. Finally, he sailed across the Atlantic Ocean to reach his final destination in London on Day 79. He traveled more than 45,000 kilometers.

Glossary

novel: a fiction book

make a bet: to arrange to pay someone if you guess something incorrectly, or for a person to pay you if you guess something correctly

journey: travel over a large distance

bound for: going to a specific place

3 Write 1, 2 or 3 to indicate the correct paragraph.

1. This paragraph is a description of Michael Palin's trip. ____
2. This paragraph gives background information on Michael Palin. ____
3. This paragraph gives information in chronological order. ____
4. This paragraph introduces the book *Around the World in 80 Days*. ____

4 Read and circle T (True) or F (False).

1. Phileas Fogg lived 150 years ago. T F
2. Jules Verne wrote *Around the World in 80 Days*. T F
3. Michael followed the same route as Phileas Fogg. T F
4. He used modern forms of transportation. T F
5. He traveled from Greece to Italy. T F
6. It took 64 days to reach Japan. T F
7. Michael's journey took less than 80 days. T F

5 🎧²⁸ **Listen and number the photos.**

6 🎧²⁸ **Listen again and circle the correct option.**

1. What exactly is virtual **travel** / **reality**?
2. If you turn your **head** / **headset**, the image moves.
3. Some governments make **simulations** / **virtual tours** of famous landmarks.
4. But can you **find** / **buy** one of these devices?
5. You can **turn** / **make** your phone into a virtual reality device…

Stop and Think! What are the advantages and disadvantages of virtual travel?

Glossary

headset: a device you wear on your head

simulation: a re-creation of specific circumstances, often for training

relive: experience something again

cardboard: thick paper, often brown and used for boxes

Culture

1 Read and match.

1. Sri Lanka is a small island
2. The country has the oldest
3. Cinnamon, a popular spice,
4. Sri Lanka is the world's largest
5. The national sport of Sri Lanka
6. A popular Sri Lankan dish is

is volleyball.
in the Indian Ocean.
rice and curry.
flag in the world.
exporter of tea.
originated in Sri Lanka.

Sri Lanka

2 Read and mark (✓) the correct option.

Shipwreck Diving

The country of Sri Lanka has a unique geographical position along one of the world's major shipping routes from East to West. For hundreds of years, ships have sailed this route. Many of these ships have sunk near the Sri Lankan coast because of storms, bad navigation and wars. Today, there are over 200 shipwrecks off the coast of Sri Lanka—and many are **unexplored**. Some of the wrecks are easy for **divers** to reach—only 30 or 40 meters below the surface—and the water is very clear. For this reason, shipwreck diving has become a popular tourist activity in Sri Lanka. After a three-day diving course, tourists can dive to see a real shipwreck.

What can you see when you dive to a shipwreck? Marine life. When a ship sinks, coral starts to cover the structure. Other creatures and fish follow, creating an artificial coral reef. For divers, the experience of diving down to the wreck and seeing the different plants and fish is **unforgettable**.

Visiting a shipwreck is also an excellent way to experience history. Many of the ships have fascinating stories. For example, marine archaeologists have discovered a wreck off the town of Godavaya. It's over 2,000 years old and full of ancient artifacts. Another shipwreck is the *HMS Hermes*, the world's first **aircraft carrier**. It sank in 1942 during the Second World War. It is in excellent condition, and it is very popular with divers.

Unfortunately, shipwrecks are also in danger. Some people visit the shipwrecks to salvage metal: they use explosives to cut apart ships, so that they can sell the metal. This destroys the marine environment, kills the fish there, and erases history. ▼

Guess What!

The official capital of Sri Lanka is Sri Jayawardenapura Kotte, or Kotte for short. It is near the city of Colombo, the business capital of the country.

To learn more about Sri Lanka's shipwrecks, go to www.divesrilanka.com

90

1. There are a lot of shipwrecks off the coast of Sri Lanka because…
   ☐ the currents near the island are dangerous.
   ☐ the island is near a major shipping route.

2. Shipwrecks have become a popular attraction because…
   ☐ they are easy for divers to reach.
   ☐ there are sharks and whales near the wrecks.

3. Shipwrecks are a great place to view…
   ☐ ancient temples and artifacts.
   ☐ coral, fish and other marine life.

4. Some people visit the shipwrecks because…
   ☐ they are interested in history.
   ☐ they want to become better divers.

5. Shipwrecks are in danger because…
   ☐ people salvage metal from the wrecks.
   ☐ violent storms are destroying the wrecks.

3 🎧²⁹ **Listen and complete the notes.**

Description of an Auto Rickshaw
- _____ wheels
- metal body and **canvas roof**
- _____ passengers

Advantages of Auto Rickshaws
- _____ than a car
- _____ enough for **narrow** country roads
- works well in _____

Disadvantages of Auto Rickshaws
- not _____
- cause _____
- make a lot of noise

4 Read and answer. What do people in Sri Lanka call auto rickshaws?

_____

 Stop and Think! What adventurous activities can world travelers do in your country?

Glossary

unexplored: not explored

divers: people who go under water, often with special equipment

unforgettable: very memorable; you cannot forget it

aircraft carrier: a military ship that carries airplanes

canvas: strong waterproof fabric

roof: the covering of a house or vehicle

narrow: not wide

1 Look and classify the activities for each destination.

 swim in the ocean

1. A Tropical Beach

_____

_____

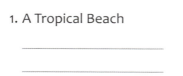

 sail

 find a treasure

2. The Old West

_____

_____

 ride horses

 mine for gold

3. A Pirate Ship

_____

_____

 stay at a five star hotel

2 🎧³⁰ Listen and mark (✓) the destination.

3 Look at the Travel Experience poster on page 93. What is the destination?
- ☐ A ski resort in the Alps
- ☐ A jousting tournament in the Middle Ages
- ☐ A city in the ancient Roman Empire

4 Read and circle the correct option.
1. The destination is **real** / **historical** / **fictional**.
2. The main event is a **tour of secret tunnels** / **jousting tournament**.
3. The poster gives **one example** / **two examples** of foods to eat.
4. The poster **mentions** / **doesn't mention** where visitors will stay.

5 Design a Travel Experience poster.
1. Choose a destination. It can be a real place like New Zealand, a historical setting like ancient Rome or even a fictional place like Middle Earth from *Lord of the Rings*.
2. Research the destination. Pick a main attraction for travelers to experience: What can visitors see or do at that attraction?
3. Plan food and accommodations: What will travelers eat? Where will they stay?
4. Make a poster and present your travel experience to the class.

Visit Medieval England! Enjoy a Jousting Tournament!

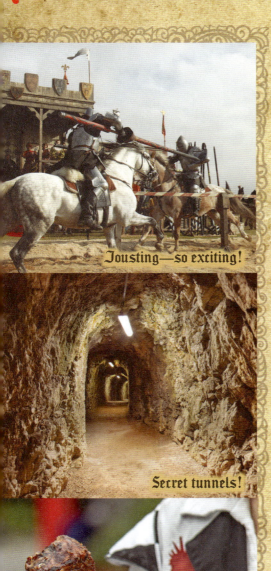
Jousting—so exciting!

Dover Castle!

Jousting was a popular sport in Europe in the Middle Ages. If you go back to the 1100s, you can attend a jousting tournament. When you arrive, you will stay at our luxury accommodations in Dover Castle! It is one of the largest castles in England. Eat in the Great Hall in the presence of the King Henry II. Don't forget to bring a knife—forks won't become popular for two hundred years! But don't worry! If you forget, another guest might share his with you. Or just eat a big turkey leg! Before the tournament, you will have time to explore the secret tunnels around Dover Castle. But save some energy for the main event: there is a lot to see at the tournament. Watch colorful processions with flags and trumpet players. Listen to musicians sing and tell stories. For jousting, knights ride horses and wear heavy, metal armor. They try to hit each other with long lances. It's a dangerous sport, but very exciting to see!

Secret tunnels!

Musicians in costumes!

A turkey leg! Mmm!

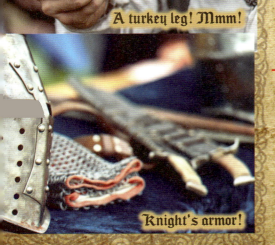
Knight's armor!

Colorful processions!

Review

1 Look and complete the travel activities.

1. _____ a flight
2. _____ a train
3. _____ in a hotel
4. _____ a passport
5. _____ a guide
6. _____ money
7. _____ a suitcase

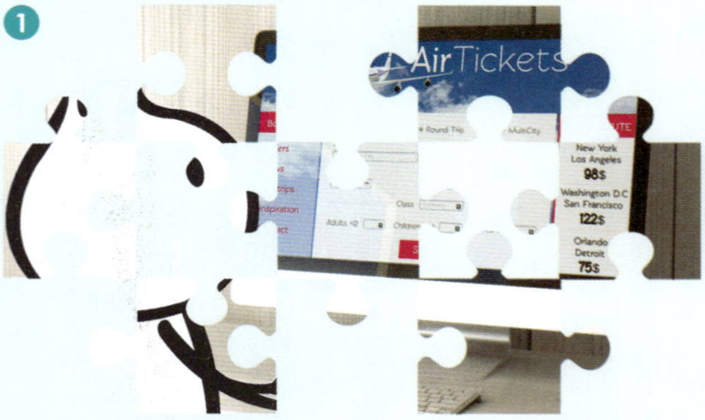

2 Look and circle the correct option.

 get hot / get hungry

 get started / get thirsty

 get there / get lost

 get up / get ready

3 Look and write the past participle form of the verbs.

 eat – _____

 give – _____

 make – _____

 hear – _____

 take – _____

 see – _____

4 Unscramble the sentences.

1. has / Bryan / Japan / been / to _____
2. for / studied / the / Karen / hasn't / test _____
3. ever / letter / you / a / have / written / ? _____
4. have / gone / to / ever / you / concert / a / ? _____

5 Look and write the sentences using the present perfect.

1. we / have lunch / already

   _____

2. she / not be / to the museum / yet

   _____

3. he / take / the test / already

   _____

4. they / not see / the movie / yet

   _____

5. you / do / your chores / yet / ?

   _____

Just for Fun

1 Find and circle eight words that form expressions with *get*.

hot   hungry   lost   ready   started   there   thirsty   up

```
N D F O T V T J Y T Q X D Z G Y
F A U K H Q H U N H Y H L F X R
S H L B I I E W E T P J O B H G
T L L G R L R J X B R Z C T H N
A O F R S X E D D R E J B V F U
R S F U T E Y E E Q A G B R Q H
T T Z B Y R R K I C D T I R E D
E Y S K G O I R A O Y Q W I W C
D Q O N B X Y U P L Q A N G R Y
```

2 Find six new words that form expressions with *get*. Then complete.

get...

a___gry

b___r___d

c___ ___d

f___ ___l

t___ ___ed

w___t

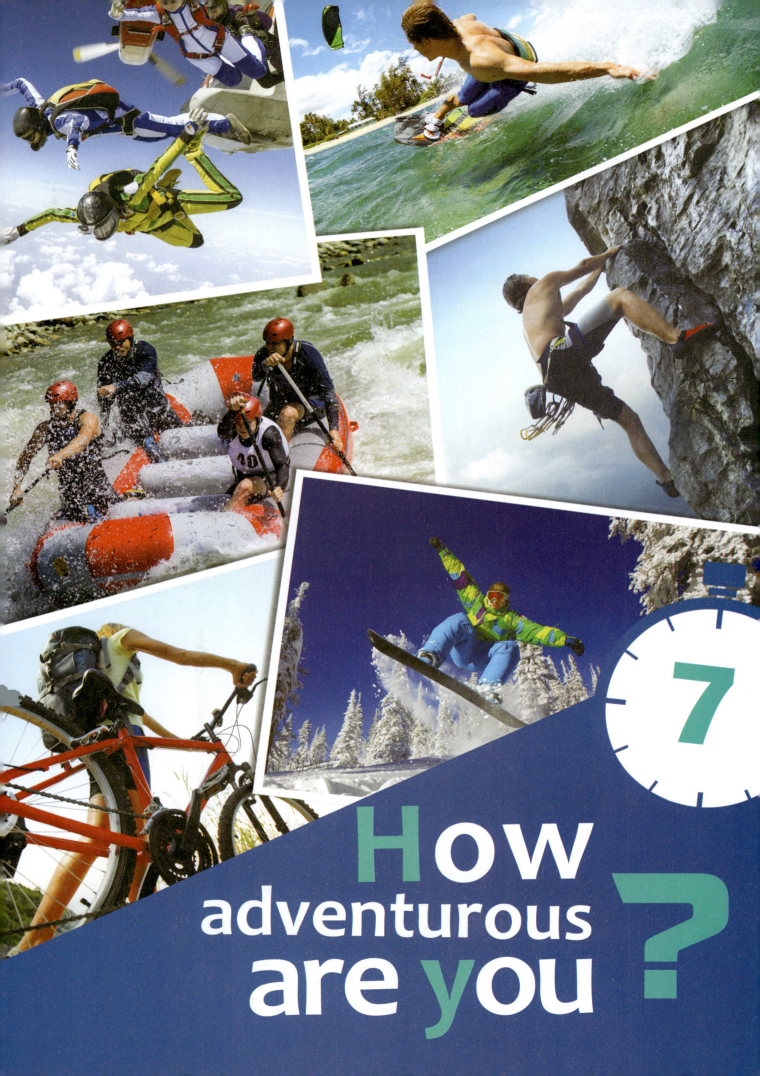

Vocabulary

1 🎧³¹ **Listen and number the extreme sports.**

rock climbing   kite surfing   snowboarding

mountain biking   skydiving   white water rafting

2 Look and write the name of the extreme sport.

① _____ ② _____

③ _____ ④ _____

⑤ _____ ⑥ _____

3 🎧³¹ Listen again and complete.

> boring   exciting   interesting   terrifying   thrilling   tiring

1. It's really _____ —your heart beats fast and you forget about everything else.

2. You see a lot of _____ places when you go mountain biking.

3. It's never _____. Every mountain is different.

4. My mom thinks skydiving is _____ ... She's extremely afraid of heights.

5. It's _____ to be in the middle of a river navigating the currents.

6. You have to train a lot because climbing can be very _____.

4 Think Fast! Describe the extreme sports using the adjectives in Activity 3.

I think white water rafting is terrifying. I'm afraid of water.

5 Look and label.

> bored   excited   interested   terrified   thrilled   tired

_____ _____ _____ _____ _____ _____

6 Read and match.

1. Jo is bored because
2. He's excited because
3. He's interested in
4. He's terrified of
5. He's thrilled about
6. He's tired because

his favorite team is winning.
a new book from the library.
winning a sports car!
he's waiting in a long line.
he did a lot of chores.
a giant spider.

7 Think Fast! Complete the table.

boring		interesting		thrilling	
	excited		terrified		tired

Grammar

1 🎧³² **Look at the Wild Adventures Survival Courses brochure. Then listen and circle T (True) or F (False).**

Wild Adventures Survival Courses

Junior Survivor
Difficulty Level: All
Ages: 8 – 15
Learn how to have fun, stay safe and protect the forest.

Island Survivor
Difficulty Level: All
Ages: 12 and up
Learn survival skills on an **uninhabited** tropical island! Find fresh water, catch fish and build a fire.

Mountain Adventurer
Difficulty Level: Experienced
Ages: 15 and up
Practice your survival skills in the mountains! Find out which plants are safe to eat, build a waterproof shelter and cook fresh **game** over a fire.

Jungle Explorer
Difficulty Level: Expert
Ages: 18 and up
Survive a trip through the jungle. Use trees and plants to construct a **raft** and then navigate through the jungle on white water **rapids**.

Might
We use the modal *might* before verbs to indicate possibility:
I **might** take the Island Survivor course.
The negative form also indicates possibility:
I **might not** sign up this year.

1. Tyler has already taken a survival course. T F
2. Megan is taking the Jungle Explorer course this year. T F
3. Tyler hasn't decided which course to take. T F
4. He might take the Mountain Adventurer course. T F
5. Megan recommends the Island Survivor course. T F
6. Megan definitely can't take a course this year. T F

2 **Read and mark (✓) about you. Then calculate your Survival IQ.**

Survival IQ

1 Would you eat a bug?

☐ Yes, I would. ☐ I might. ☐ No, I wouldn't.

In Western countries, people often think bugs are disgusting, but in other parts of the world, people eat them every day. They're very high in protein. Go ahead and take a bite! Just make sure you know which bugs are safe to eat!

✓ = 25 points   +/– = 15 points   – = 5 points

2 Would you drink water from a lake or river?

☐ Yes, I would. ☐ I might. ☐ No, I wouldn't.

If you are lost in the forest, or worse—in the desert—your most important resource is clean water. You should always carry water when you go hiking. Don't drink from a lake or river. It might have dangerous bacteria or parasites that could make you very sick.

✓ = 5 points   +/– = 10 points   – = 25 points

Present Perfect: Never

I've **never** been very adventurous.
He's **never** gone skydiving.

3 🎧³³ Listen and mark (✓ or ✗) the activities that each person has done.

- go bungee jumping ☐
- swim with sharks ☐
- touch a spider ☐
- see a tornado ☐

4 Write sentences about Tara and Mike using the present perfect.

1. _____
2. _____
3. _____
4. _____

5 Think Fast! In your notebook, write four sentences about things you have never done. (2 min)

Glossary

uninhabited: with no people living there
game: wild animals that you eat
raft: a simple boat
rapids: a part of a river with rocks and strong currents
bug: an insect

---

3 Would you run away from a bear?

☐ Yes, I would.   ☐ I might.   ☐ No, I wouldn't.

Actually, running from a bear is a terrible idea. Why? Because bears can run faster than you can. They can also climb trees. If you see a bear, or any other large animal, you should try to scare the animal: shout, jump and wave your arms. If you're lucky, the animal will run away.

+ = 0 points   +/– = 0 points   – = 25 points

4 Would you eat wild berries?

☐ Yes, I would.   ☐ I might.   ☐ No, I wouldn't.

Imagine that you're in the forest and you haven't eaten in two days. You see some delicious-looking red berries. What do you do? If you aren't 100% certain that they're safe to eat, you should not eat them. Some berries are very toxic.

+ = 10 points   +/– = 20 points   – = 25 points

5 Would you take a compass and a map?

☐ Yes, I would!   ☐ I might.   ☐ No, I wouldn't.

Nowadays, with maps on our phones and GPS trackers, you might want to leave the compass and paper map at home. That is a bad idea. Devices can get wet, broken or lost. If you are in the wilderness, you need a compass and a map to navigate, and you should know how to use them.

+ = 25 points   +/– = 15 points   – = 5 points

Would

Would you eat a bug?
Yes, I **would**!
No, I **wouldn't**.

Scores:

125 points: You're a Survival Genius! You know some important facts to stay safe in nature.

85 – 120 points: Not too bad... Maybe you should take a survival course.

25 – 80 points: You should explore nature more, but take an experienced guide with you!

Reading & Writing

> **Be Strategic!**
> Understanding text organization can make you a better reader *and* writer. Each paragraph is a category of information. If you can classify information, you can write a clear, organized text.

1 Look and classify the words.

tiger   school   scared
sad   face   lion
supermarket   angry
elephant   museum
hands
arms   zebra
library
happy
feet

Zoo Animals
▶ 102 _____
_____
_____
_____

City Places
_____
_____
_____

Emotions
_____
_____
_____

Body Parts
_____
_____
_____

2 Read and number the headings.
☐ Animals as Transportation ☐ Technology and Transportation
☐ The **Roots** of Human Exploration

Animals and Adventure

¹ Modern technology has improved transportation and our ability to explore. We can send **space probes** to distant planets and submarines to the deepest parts of the ocean. We can zoom around the world on planes and high-speed trains. Buses and subways carry commuters through cities, and cars take us to our many destinations—even without humans driving them!

² Just a century ago, transportation often involved animals. **Oxen** pulled farmers' **plows** and wagons. Horses carried people from place to place. **Mules** pulled canal boats and mine cars full of coal. But they weren't the only animals used for transportation. Travelers have used camels, ideally suited for the desert, for hundreds of years. Some call them "ships of the desert." In India and Thailand, elephants were useful for transportation, while in the arctic, dogs and reindeer pulled sleds in the snow.

³ Long before humans used animals as transportation, animals influenced human migration. In fact, this might be the reason why humans became so adventurous. For thousands of years, across Africa, Asia, Europe and the Americas, humans followed the animals that were their food: fish, buffalo, bison—even mammoths. Later, humans developed agriculture, but they still moved with their animals—sheep, goats and cattle—across plains and deserts. The cowboys herded cattle from the American West to railroad towns to feed cities across the country. Animals are still an important part of transportation in some places, and if you have the opportunity to explore, you might get to see a dog sled or ride an elephant. Just remember that you probably have animals to thank for being an adventurer in the first place.

3 Read again. Underline names of working animals and circle names of food animals.

4 Imagine you need to add facts to the article. Circle the correct option.

1. helicopters — Paragraph 1 — Paragraph 2 — Paragraph 3
2. horses that carried soldiers — Paragraph 1 — Paragraph 2 — Paragraph 3
3. the first humans in North America — Paragraph 1 — Paragraph 2 — Paragraph 3
4. travel to the moon — Paragraph 1 — Paragraph 2 — Paragraph 3

5 Classify the facts for an article about sled dogs. Write *B* (Basic Facts) or *H* (History).

1. Huskies and malamutes are the most common breeds of sled dog. _____
2. People started using dog sleds 3,000 years ago in arctic regions. _____
3. Dog sleds were the main form of winter transportation until the mid 20th century. _____
4. Dogs traveled from northern Asia to North America with humans. _____
5. Sled dogs can run 30 km per hour. _____
6. Their favorite food is reindeer meat. _____

6 In your notebook, write two paragraphs about sled dogs using the facts in Activity 5.

Stop and Think! Is it OK to use animals for food and/or work? Why or why not?

Glossary

roots: the parts of a plant in soil; the origins of a person or thing

space probes: machines that collect information in space

oxen: two or more cows that pull a wagon or farm equipment

plows: farm equipment for digging and moving soil

mules: working animals; a combination of a horse and a donkey

Culture

1 🎧³⁴ **Read and guess. Then listen and circle the correct option.**

1. Antarctica is in the **northern** / **southern** hemisphere.

2. Antarctica is **half** / **twice** the size of Australia.

3. Most of the continent is covered in 1.6 kilometers of **snow** / **ice**.

4. Antarctica is the world's largest **desert** / **island**.

5. **Summer** / **Winter** in Antarctica begins in December.

6. Around **1,000** / **4,000** people—mostly scientists—live in Antarctica in the summer months.

7. In the winter, it is **sunny** / **dark** for 24 hours a day.

2 Look and label the map.

- Africa
- Australia
- Atlantic Ocean
- Indian Ocean
- Pacific Ocean
- South America

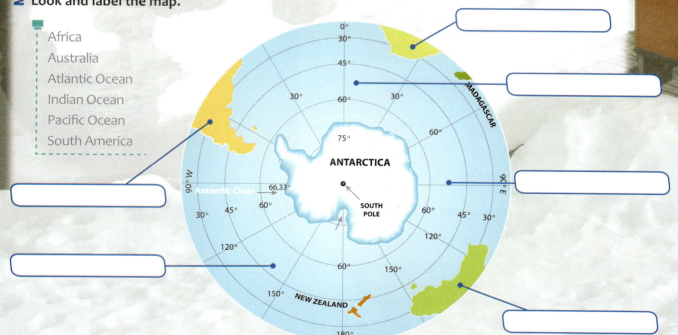

3 Read the article and write A (Amundsen) or S (Scott).

The Race to the South Pole

In 1910, two teams of explorers set out on the **ultimate** adventure to become the first people to **reach** the South Pole. It was a very dangerous trip. The total distance to the South Pole and back to safety was nearly 3,000 kilometers. They needed to cross mountains and glaciers, and the average temperature was around -30°C.

One team was led by Roald Amundsen, a Norwegian explorer. Amundsen learned about arctic survival from Inuit people, and other team members had experience living in extreme arctic conditions. They planned to use skis and dog sleds to travel across Antarctica to reach the South Pole.

The other team was led by Robert F. Scott, a British captain who had explored Antarctica in an earlier expedition. His plan was to use mostly horses and **motorized** sleds to get to the South Pole.

Amundsen's team set out for the South Pole on October 20, 1911, and they arrived on December 14th. They returned safely to their base camp on January 26, 1912.

Scott's team set out November 1, 1911. They struggled with the horses and the motorized sleds, but they did reach the South Pole on January 17, 1912. They found a tent full of **supplies** and a note from Amundsen. They were not the first team at the South Pole! **Tragically**, on the return trip, the temperatures dropped to -40°C and they all died in a snowstorm only 18 kilometers from their base camp.

Robert F. Scott and his team were seen as great heroes. The scientific research from Scott's Terra Nova Expedition established Antarctica as a research site for many different areas of study including geology, biology and meteorology.

1. He led two Antarctic expeditions. _____
2. He was British. _____
3. He was Norwegian. _____
4. He was familiar with Inuit survival skills. _____
5. He used skis and dog sleds. _____
6. He used horses and motorized sleds. _____
7. He was first to reach the South Pole. _____
8. He led the Terra Nova Expedition. _____

4 Underline the dates in the article. Then complete the timeline.

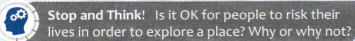

Amundsen sets out
Amundsen reaches the South Pole
Amundsen reaches base camp
Scott sets out
Scott reaches the South Pole

Stop and Think! Is it OK for people to risk their lives in order to explore a place? Why or why not?

Glossary
ultimate: the best
reach: to arrive at
motorized: with a motor
supplies: necessary items, often food
tragically: sadly

Project

1 Look at the Adventure Profile on page 107. What was the adventure?

2 Read and underline the Adventure Profile facts in the article.

After high school, many young people wait a year before going to college. Some work, some volunteer and some travel. Tom Davies, a nineteen-year-old from London, decided to cycle around the world!

To prepare, Tom spent several months training. He did a lot of exercise in the gym and also rode his bicycle on difficult terrains. He was very careful about which items to pack. He couldn't take many things, just some clothing, a phone, a laptop and a repair kit for his bike. He didn't take a tent. He planned to stay in hotels. (His parents helped with the expenses.)

For the first part of his trip, Tom went through France, Italy, Albania and Greece all the way to Istanbul, in Turkey. Then he flew to Mumbai and cycled across India. His next stop was Myanmar, and then Vietnam. From there, he cycled to Thailand and Singapore. He flew to Australia to cycle across the country and after that, New Zealand. He flew to San Francisco, in the United States, and cycled north to Canada. He flew to Spain, then cycled north through France, home to London.

Tom Davies cycled a total of 46,620 kilometers in 174 days. Most of the journey went well, but he did have a few challenges: food poisoning in Italy, bad weather, being chased by dogs in Albania and a group of monkeys in India. Tom became the youngest person to cycle around the world and he raised $80,000 for charity.

3 ^35 Listen and circle the correct option.

Adventurer: **Jonathan** / **Jessica** Meir
Age: **28** / **38** years old
Transportation: spacecraft
Distance: 54.6 **million** / **billion** kilometers
Places: the US, France, **Korea** / **Canada**, Antarctica, Belize
Preparation: astronaut training, learning **Japanese** / **Russian**
Challenges: living in a dangerous environment, being away from family
Achievements: She has become a marine biologist, a pilot and an **artist** / **astronaut**.
Future Plans: She plans to accept any mission NASA gives her. She might be one of the first humans on **the Moon** / **Mars**.

4 Choose and research an adventurer. Make an Adventure Profile.

Laura Dekker	Jordan Romero	Jade Hameister	Dashiel Alsup	Trinity Arsenault

ADVENTURE PROFILE

NAME: Tom Davies

AGE: 19 years old

PLACES VISITED: France, Italy, Albania, Greece, Turkey, India, Myanmar, Vietnam, Thailand, Singapore, Australia, New Zealand, the US, Canada, Spain

TRANSPORTATION: bicycle, airplane

TRAVEL DISTANCE: 46,620 kilometers

PREPARATION ACTIVITIES: exercising, riding his bike on difficult terrain

CHALLENGES: food poisoning, bad weather, dogs, monkeys

ACHIEVEMENTS: He was the youngest person to cycle around the world. He raised $80,000 for charity.

Review

1 Look and label the extreme sports.

1. _____   2. _____   3. _____

4. _____   5. _____   6. _____

2 Read and circle the correct option.

1. The movie about the vampire was **terrified** / **terrifying**.
2. We were very **tired** / **tiring** after we did all of our chores.
3. The hot air balloon trip was **thrilled** / **thrilling**!
4. The children were **excited** / **exciting** about their visit to the zoo.
5. I was **bored** / **boring** waiting for my flight, so I read a magazine.
6. I read an **interested** / **interesting** article about hiking in Europe.

3 Complete the sentences using the unused words from Activity 2.

1. The new action movie was _____. You should see it!
2. To apply for the scholarship, you need to complete a lot of _____ forms.
3. Cycling across the country was very _____. Next time, I'm flying!
4. He was _____ when his parents gave him a new car.
5. My brother is really _____ in Manga.
6. My mom was _____ when she saw a mouse in the kitchen.

4 Read and correct the sentences.

1. I might going to the gym this afternoon.
   _____
2. We might not to go to the party tomorrow.
   _____
3. My family is might travel to Spain this summer.
   _____
4. She might has basketball practice after school.
   _____

5 **Look and write the questions using *would*. Then answer about you.**

ride in an auto rickshaw

_____

Yes, I would.   No, I wouldn't.

eat street food

_____

Yes, I would.   No, I wouldn't.

go on a cruise

_____

Yes, I would.   No, I wouldn't.

drink yak's milk

_____

Yes, I would.   No, I wouldn't.

6 **Look and write about Gianna and Quinn using the present perfect and *never*.**

	win a race	take a dance class	fail a test	go sailing	fly in a plane
Gianna	✓	✓	✗	✗	✓
Quinn	✗	✗	✓	✓	✓

1. _____
2. _____
3. _____
4. _____

Just for Fun

1 Look and write the extreme sports.

❶

❷

❸

_____

_____

_____

❹

❺

❻

_____

_____

_____

2 Look and complete.

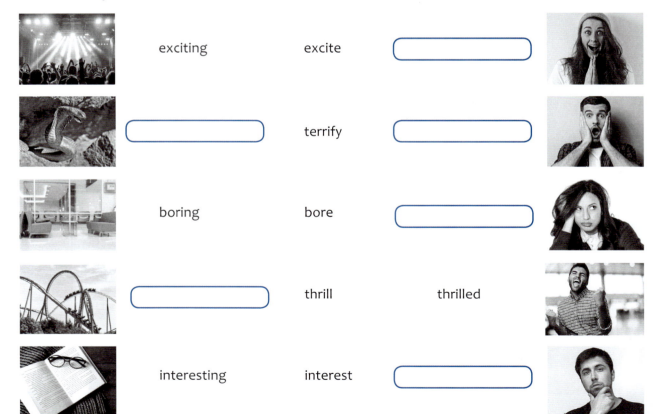

	exciting	excite		
		terrify		
	boring	bore		
		thrill	thrilled	
	interesting	interest		
		tire	tired	

Vocabulary

1. 🎧³⁶ **Listen and write J (Jaya), B (Bryan) or M (Maia). Which activities do they do?**

Tell Your Story

Assignment #248: How do you spend your time?
Here are some example activities to get you started:

| stream movies | go out to eat | stay up late | work out |
| keep a journal | hang out | sleep in | order take-out |

Jaya

"I stream movies on my computer..."

Bryan

"I do farm chores in the morning before school..."

Maia

"...I want to be a writer so I keep a journal..."

2. 🎧³⁶ **Listen again and circle the correct option.**

1. Jaya streams movies or TV series with her **brother** / **sister** Adya.
2. They do that on **weekends** / **weekdays**.
3. Bryan plays **basketball** / **football** with his friends.
4. To work out, he **lifts weights** / **goes jogging**.
5. Maia loves ordering **Mexican** / **Chinese** take-out.
6. On the weekends, she sleeps in until **ten** / **eleven** o'clock.

3 Read and match.

1. keep a journal   spend time with people
2. stream movies   exercise
3. order take-out   watch online movies
4. go out to eat   go to a restaurant and eat there
5. stay up late   buy food at a restaurant to eat at home
6. sleep in   sleep extra time in the morning
7. work out   go to bed very late
8. hang out   write your thoughts and experiences in a notebook

4 Read and complete using vocabulary items from Activity 3.

Free time was very different 100 years ago. In the early 20th century, people definitely didn't (1) _____ movies or (2) _____ take-out. People did (3) _____ out to eat, but it was often very formal, and not as common as nowadays. Many people worked six or seven days a week, so sleeping (4) _____ was not an option either. However, keeping a (5) _____ was pretty common. People often wrote letters to friends, too. Hanging (6) _____ has always been popular, but back then, you might have a picnic or ride bikes with friends. People didn't usually stay (7) _____ late because many homes didn't have electricity, and there weren't many activities to do in the evening. People did (8) _____ out, though. There were even exercise machines to help people get in shape!

5 Read and circle Y (Yes) or N (No).

A hundred years ago, did people…

1. hang out?   Y   N
2. order take-out?   Y   N
3. stream movies?   Y   N
4. work out?   Y   N
5. keep a journal?   Y   N
6. go out to eat?   Y   N
7. sleep in?   Y   N
8. stay up late?   Y   N

6 Think Fast! Which activities do you usually do? Make a list in your notebook.

Grammar

1 Read and mark (✓) the correct option.

Dear Campers,
The welcome ceremony is at **4 p.m.** at the picnic area. Come and meet the other campers and enjoy some snacks and drinks.
See you there!
Sincerely,
Pamela Jacobs
Camp Director

1. What is the activity?
   ☐ a birthday   ☐ a field trip   ☐ summer camp
2. What is at 4 o'clock?
   ☐ a welcome ceremony   ☐ dinner   ☐ a fishing class
3. Who can campers meet there?
   ☐ other campers   ☐ their relatives   ☐ camp instructors
4. What else can campers do at the event?
   ☐ play music   ☐ sing songs   ☐ eat snacks

2 Read and complete the dialogues. Then underline the sentences with *too* and *either*.

> been   but   from   have   meet   where

Alex: Hi. I'm Alex.
Laura: I'm Laura. Nice to _____ you.
Alex: _____ are you from?
Laura: Colorado. You?
Alex: I'm _____ Colorado too!
Laura: _____ you been to this camp before?
Alex: No, I've never _____ here.
Laura: I've never been here either. _____ it looks pretty cool.

3 Read and circle the correct option.

1. - We just arrived yesterday.
   - I just got here **too / either**.

2. - I don't like waking up early.
   - I don't like it much **too / either**.

3. - I'm not good at fishing.
   - I'm not **too / either**, but they'll help us.

4. - I love cooking on a campfire!
   - I do **too / either**!

Too, Either

We can express similar opinions or circumstances using *too* and *either*:
➕ I like camping **too**.
➖ I don't like fishing **either**.

4 Think Fast! In your notebook, write a dialogue using *too* and *either*.

5 🎧³⁷ **Listen and complete the infographic.**

So, Neither

We can also use expressions with *So* and *Neither* to express similar opinions or circumstances:
- I swim well. - **So** do I.
- She can't sing. - **Neither** can I.

6 🎧³⁸ **Listen and match.**

1. I do a lot of outdoor activities.   I don't either.
2. No, I don't.   So do I.
3. I read at least an hour a day.   Neither do I.
4. I don't listen to music.   I do too.

7 Read and complete the responses.

1. I don't like hot weather.   Neither _____.
2. We have a test tomorrow.   So _____.
3. I can't swim.   Neither _____.
4. I am really interested in yoga.   So _____.
5. I'm not a fan of horror movies.   Neither _____.

Guess What!
Always check what verb is used in the first sentence so that you use the correct auxiliary in your response.

Listening & Reading

1 🎧³⁹ **Listen and number the speakers.**

Dr. Stephens   Dustin   Lynn   Martin   Ms. Wagner   Sophie

> **Be Strategic!**
> Identifying speakers can help you to understand a situation better.

"What do you think the definition of bullying is?" ☐

"Bullying is when other kids say bad things about you or laugh at you." ☐

"You should tell someone, but… no one really does." ☐

_____ _____ _____

"Some bullying is **physical**, when others try to hurt you or break your **stuff**." ☐

"What should you do if you see or experience bullying?" ☐

"What about when other kids **exclude** you from a group?" ☐

_____ _____ _____

2 🎧³⁹ **Listen again and write the names.**

3 Read and match.

1. Dr. Stephens is   what to do about bullying.
2. Ms. Wagner is   a psychologist.
3. Sophie offers   what usually happens.
4. Dustin talks about   physical bullying.
5. Lynn wants to know   a teacher.
6. Martin explains   to be a friend.
7. Sophie, Dustin, Lynn and Martin   are students.
8. A solution is   a definition of bullying.

4 **Read the blog and write the headings.**

A Big Move!   I'm on the Team!   Whew! A Long Week

September 12th –

It's hard to believe it, but I've been here for three weeks. The time has passed really fast and I've already made some friends. Classes are going well, and I'm starting to feel like I know my way around. This school is different from my old school because it's very diverse. There are kids from Asia, Latin America and Africa. One of my best friends is from Somalia. His name is Nadif! And… Soccer tryouts went great! I just found out that I'm on the soccer team. Practice starts this week!

By David | 5 Comments | Read More >

August 29th –

I just finished my first week at my new school. Things are going well. I miss my old friends, but people here are OK. Since I'm a new student, the school assigned me a partner—Jarred—and he's helping me **get used to** the school. Some kids started making fun of my red hair. It wasn't a big deal, but Jarred and some of his friends told them to stop. And one of my classmates invited me to her birthday party this weekend. It'll be a good chance to meet some people!

By David | 1 Comments | Read More >

July 27th –

Well, it's official: I'm going to a new school in the fall. My dad has a new job and we're moving to a different city. The good thing is my sister is going to the same school, so at least I'll know someone. Yesterday I said good-bye to my friends. We agreed to keep in touch. It shouldn't be too hard with social media, but it's not the same as being there. I saw the webpage for the new school and it looks good. They have a soccer team. I can't wait for **tryouts**. My sister wants to play volleyball. I'm excited, but a little nervous.

5 **Read and circle T (True) or F (False).**

1. David moved to a different country.   T   F
2. His sister is going to college.   T   F
3. He looked at the school's webpage.   T   F
4. Everyone has treated David well.   T   F
5. Jarred doesn't have any friends.   T   F
6. The school is very diverse.   T   F
7. David's new best friend is from Africa.   T   F
8. Soccer practice starts soon.   T   F

 Stop and Think!   How can friendship prevent bullying?

Glossary

physical: involving the body or real objects

stuff: things

exclude: to not allow someone to participate

tryouts: a test of abilities in order to be on a team

get used to: to get accustomed to; to adapt

Culture

1 Read and number the photos.

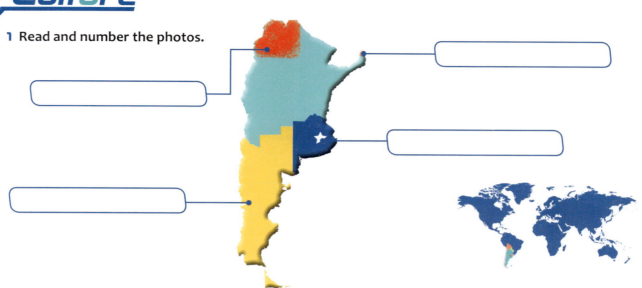

Argentina

There are many different places that make up the country of Argentina. Argentina has the Andes Mountains in the west and the Atlantic Ocean along the eastern coast. It stretches 3,694 kilometers from north to south.

1. Iguazu Falls is located in the north of Argentina on the border with Brazil. There are 275 individual waterfalls! The falls are a part of a jungle ecosystem.

2. Patagonia is an area in the south of Argentina and the neighboring country of Chile. Not a lot of people live there, but many people visit to see its snowy mountain landscapes.

3. The northeast region of Argentina is a high **altitude** desert called the Puna de Atacama. Many people go rock climbing there.

4. The capital city, Buenos Aires, is in the east of the country. It is on the Atlantic Coast near Uruguay.

2 Read again and label the map.

3 🎧⁴⁰ Read and guess. Then listen and circle the correct option.

1. There are **penguins** / **turtles** in Argentina.
2. Argentina means "**Country** / **Land** of Silver."
3. *Gauchos* are Argentinean **cowboys** / **boots**.
4. *Yerba mate* is a traditional **drink** / **food**.
5. **The tango** / **Salsa** is a dance from Argentina.
6. *Dulce de leche* is made with milk and **salt** / **sugar**.

4 **Read and complete the text.**

- became
- groups
- important
- introduced
- like
- million
- others
- people
- President
- stores

When the Spanish came to the Americas in the 16th century, they brought (1) _____ from Spain to live in Argentina. These new settlers added to the indigenous peoples of the region. When the country (2) _____ independent in 1818, more Europeans came to Argentina. There were immigrants from Spain, Italy, France, Germany and Britain. (3) _____ came from Russia and Eastern Europe. Many Jewish people came to Argentina to escape **persecution**. The population jumped from only four (4) _____ in 1895 to 16 million just fifty years later. This was not an accident. In fact, the government of Argentina invited immigrants to the country because there was a lot of land and not many people.

Argentina has a very unique culture because of all of these immigrants. Italian foods (5) _____ pasta and pizza are an (6) _____ part of Argentinean **cuisine**. British immigrants built railways and (7) _____ the sport of soccer. There is even a region in Argentina now where people speak Welsh. There was also a (8) _____ of Argentina—Carlos Menem—whose parents were Syrian immigrants! Even the accent of Argentinean Spanish is a result of the many different immigrant (9) _____. Nowadays, there are many immigrants from Asia. There are neighborhoods in Buenos Aires where you can find authentic Chinese and Korean restaurants and (10) _____. Immigration continues to **enrich** and transform the country.

5 **Read and match.**

1. The Spanish were
2. In the 1800s, immigrants
3. The Argentinean government
4. Immigration has created
5. New immigrants also

- was in favor of immigration.
- a unique and complex culture.
- enrich and transform the country.
- came from many parts of Europe.
- the first immigrants to Argentina.

 Stop and Think! What challenges do immigrants experience?

Glossary

altitude: the height of an object or place above sea level

silver: a valuable gray metal

persecution: violence or discrimination against a group of people

cuisine: the food of a specific culture

enrich: to add value to something

1 Take the Social Acceptance Survey. Write *All the time*, *Sometimes* or *Never*.

Social Acceptance Survey

1. Do you feel accepted and valued in your town / community? _____
2. Do you make jokes about members of a particular social group? _____
3. Can you be yourself around other people? _____
4. Do you criticize people for how they look or talk? _____
5. Do people treat you differently than they treat other people? _____

2 🎧⁴¹ Listen and circle for Eva's brother, Josh.

1. All the time   Sometimes   Never
2. All the time   Sometimes   Never
3. All the time   Sometimes   Never
4. All the time   Sometimes   Never
5. All the time   Sometimes   Never

3 🎧⁴² Listen and circle for Eva's neighbor, Amber.

1. All the time   Sometimes   Never
2. All the time   Sometimes   Never
3. All the time   Sometimes   Never
4. All the time   Sometimes   Never
5. All the time   Sometimes   Never

4 Look at the survey results on page 121. Circle *T* (True) or *F* (False).

1. Most people feel accepted and valued in their community.   T   F
2. No one makes jokes about members of other social groups.   T   F
3. A small percentage of people can always be themselves.   T   F
4. A lot of people criticize others sometimes.   T   F
5. No one feels like they are treated differently.   T   F

5 Do your own Social Acceptance Survey. Interview people in your community and record your results.

1. Copy the table in your notebook.
2. Interview five people. Record your results.
3. Form groups and combine your results.
4. Calculate percentages for each answer. Divide by the total number of interviews.
5. Make a report sheet with pie charts for each question.

	All the Time	Sometimes	Never
1. Do you feel accepted and valued in your town / community?	15	9	1
2. Do you make jokes about members of a particular social group?	7	12	6
3. Can you be yourself around other people?	4	14	7
4. Do you criticize people for how they look or talk?	8	15	2
5. Do people treat you differently than they treat other people?	5	11	9

Social Acceptance Survey

I interviewed five people for the social acceptance survey. Then I combined my results with other group members' results. In total, we surveyed 25 people.

1. Do you feel accepted and valued in your town / community?

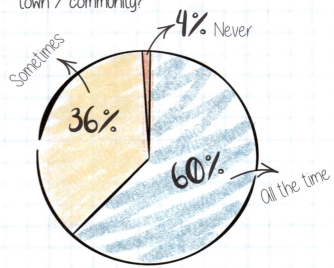

- Sometimes 36%
- Never 4%
- All the time 60%

2. Do you make jokes about members of a particular social group?

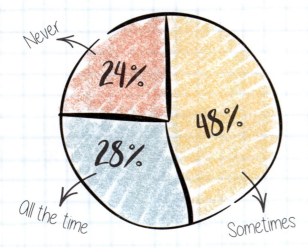

- Never 24%
- Sometimes 48%
- All the time 28%

3. Can you be yourself around other people?

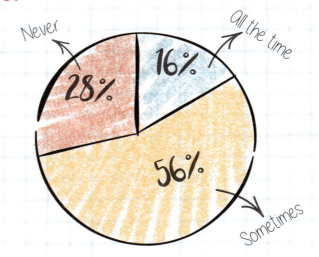

- Never 28%
- All the time 16%
- Sometimes 56%

4. Do you criticize people for how they look or talk?

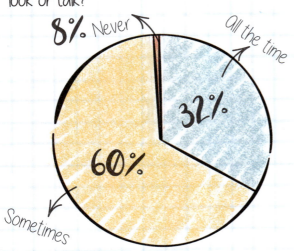

- Never 8%
- All the time 32%
- Sometimes 60%

5. Do people treat you differently than they treat other people?

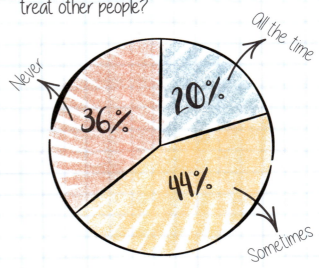

- Never 36%
- All the time 20%
- Sometimes 44%

Review

1 Look and complete the sentences.

We always _____ on the weekend.

My brother Owen _____ at the gym.

I love to _____ on my tablet.

My mom is really busy so we _____ a lot.

My sister Maggie _____.

My friends and I _____ at the park after school.

My cousins _____, but not on school nights.

Jo always _____ on Saturdays.

2 Read and complete using *too* or *either*.

Tania: Hi, Matt. I'm watching TV. What are you doing?

Matt: I'm watching TV (1) _____.

Tania: Oh, what are you watching?

Matt: It's a nature documentary, actually. I finally don't have any homework to do.

Tania: I don't have any homework (2) _____. Do you want to see a movie? I haven't seen the new Star Wars movie.

Matt: I haven't seen it (3) _____. What time does it start?

Tania: At five-thirty. I don't need to have dinner, though. I already ate.

Matt: Me (4) _____. Should we meet there?

Tania: That sounds good. See you there!

3 Read and match.

1. I love Indian food.
2. We're going shopping soon.
3. She can't swim.
4. I don't know how to cook.
5. He's not good at sports.
6. I haven't had lunch yet.

Neither do I.
Neither have I.
So do I.
Neither can I.
So are we.
Neither am I.

4 Read and answer using *Me too* or *Me neither*.

① A: I'm going on vacation next week.
B: _____.

② A: I want to go swimming in the ocean.
B: _____! And look for seashells.

③ A: I don't like long flights, though.
B: _____. But our flight is only two hours.

④ A: I already packed my suitcase!
B: _____! I like to be prepared.

⑤ A: Oh, no! I didn't pack my swimsuit!
B: _____. I'm going to buy one there.

⑥ A: I can't wait!
B: _____! I'm so excited!

Just for Fun

1. **Choose and mark (✓) one option from each set. Then use your selections to complete the silly stories.**

   1. a celebration
      - ☐ Thanksgiving
      - ☐ New Year's Eve
      - ☐ Independence Day

   2. a celebration activity
      - ☐ set off fireworks
      - ☐ watch a parade
      - ☐ wave flags

   3. a symptom or injury
      - ☐ runny nose
      - ☐ sunburn
      - ☐ stomachache

   4. an environment action
      - ☐ planting trees
      - ☐ reducing carbon emissions
      - ☐ sending garbage to landfills

   5. a fan activity
      - ☐ collect action figures
      - ☐ dress up as a character
      - ☐ get an autograph

   6. a keepsake
      - ☐ baby tooth
      - ☐ seashell
      - ☐ toy car

   7. a collocation with *get*
      - ☐ get hungry
      - ☐ get thirsty
      - ☐ get lost

   8. a habit
      - ☐ go out to eat
      - ☐ work out
      - ☐ order take-out

Silly Story 1

One day, I was _____ (AN ENVIRONMENT ACTION) when I started to _____ (A COLLOCATION WITH GET). I realized that I also had a _____ (A SYMPTOM OR INJURY). I was alone and I didn't have any money, so I decided to _____ (A CELEBRATION ACTIVITY) and sell my magic _____ (A KEEPSAKE). It worked! A man came by. He was on his way to _____ (A HABIT), so he stopped to _____ (A CELEBRATION ACTIVITY) with me. He gave me $100 for my magic _____ (A KEEPSAKE). I used the money to buy lunch and _____ (A FAN ACTIVITY). It was the best _____ (A CELEBRATION) ever!

Silly Story 2

_____ (AN ENVIRONMENT ACTION) on _____ (A CELEBRATION) isn't easy. First, you need to _____ (A HABIT). You'll probably get a _____ (A SYMPTOM OR INJURY) and you might even _____ (A COLLOCATION WITH GET). Don't worry! Just take out your phone and call a friend to help you _____ (A CELEBRATION ACTIVITY) with you. Then turn around, clap your hands and show everyone your cousin's shiny yellow _____ (A KEEPSAKE). Then you'll be able to _____ (A FAN ACTIVITY) at the supermarket.

Workbook

Unit 1

Vocabulary – Celebrations

1 Look and label.

- a cap
- candles
- open
- and
- make
- get
- a diploma
- presents
- ~~watch~~
- fireworks
- ~~wave~~
- gown
- ~~flags~~
- resolutions
- set off
- ~~a parade~~
- blow out
- wear

0a. _____wave flags_____   0b. _____watch a parade_____

1a. _____   1b. _____

2a. _____   2b. _____

3a. _____   3b. _____

2 Look and write the celebration.

0. _____Independence Day_____   1. _____

2. _____   3. _____

3 Read and complete.

athletes ~~enjoy~~ fireworks get picnic science watch

Come and (0) ___enjoy___ our Annual Sports Day on Saturday, August 27th! At noon, you can (1) _____ a parade of (2) _____. Competitions begin at 1:00 and go until 4 p.m. All athletes will (3) _____ a certificate for participation. After the competitions, stay for a (4) _____ and watch the (5) _____ club students set off (6) _____.

Guess What!
When a person graduates, say *Congratulations!* For many other occasions, we say *Happy* and the name of the event: *Happy Birthday! Happy New Year!*

Grammar – Present Continuous (future meaning)

1 Read and match.

0. We usually use the present continuous — for activities that are happening now.
1. We use the verb *be* and — add *–ing* to the end of the verb.
2. We can also use the present continuous — to talk about future plans.

2 Read and complete the dialogue.

- coming
- meeting
- ~~doing~~
- having
- going
- what
- taking

Jamie: Hey, Pete! How are you?
Pete: Fine, thanks. What are you (0) _____doing_____ after school?
Jamie: I'm (1) _____ my dog to the vet.
Pete: Oh, is he OK?
Jamie: Yes, he just really needs a bath! (2) _____ are you doing tomorrow?
Pete: I'm (3) _____ lunch with my family, but I'm free in the afternoon.
Jamie: A couple of friends and I are (4) _____ to a fireworks show tomorrow night. Do you want to come?
Pete. That's sounds great. What time are you (5) _____?
Jamie: Around 7 p.m. My sister Lucy is (6) _____, too.

3 Read and mark (✓).

	Now	Future
0. Are you coming to my party?	☐	✓
1. I'm meeting my friends for lunch.	☐	☐
2. Bruno's busy. He's studying for a test.	☐	☐
3. It's raining very hard.	☐	☐
4. Our soccer team is playing on Saturday.	☐	☐
5. When are you going on vacation?	☐	☐

4 **Complete using the correct forms of the verbs.**

0. We _____'re visiting_____ (visit) my grandparents tomorrow.
1. Julia _____ (have) a Halloween party next Friday.
2. We _____ (go) to the baseball game tonight!
3. I _____ (go) to school tomorrow.
4. Mike and Eva _____ (sing) a song at the school concert.
5. My aunt _____ (take) us to the zoo on Sunday.

5 **Write the negative forms of the sentences in Activity 4.**

0. We aren't visiting my grandparents tomorrow.
1. _____
2. _____
3. _____
4. _____
5. _____

Review

1 **Read the clues and guess the celebration activity.**

0. to extinguish small fires on a dessert _____blow out candles_____
1. to pay attention to people in a procession _____
2. to cause explosions in the sky _____
3. to have an unusual hat and robe on your body _____
4. to move symbols of a country in the air _____

2 **Unscramble and answer about you.**

0. you / doing / right / homework / now / are / ?
   Are you doing homework right now?   Yes, I am.

1. going / family / your / today / shopping / is / ?
   _____

2. dentist / the / are / you / to / tomorrow / going / ?
   _____

3. party / having / are / friends / a / this / your / weekend / ?
   _____

4. tomorrow / to / going / are / you / school / ?
   _____

Reading

1 Read and complete the facts.

First   half   languages   Navajo   ~~tribes~~

0. There are hundreds of American Indian ___tribes___ in the United States.
1. In Canada, indigenous people prefer the term _____ Nations.
2. About _____ of the states in the US have American Indian names.
3. There are 150 American Indian _____ in the US and Canada.
4. The most common indigenous language is _____.

2 Read and complete the mind map in your notebook.

A powwow was once an important **gathering** to negotiate peace between tribes. The name *powwow* comes from a similar-sounding Narragansett word for a healing ceremony. Now the word powwow refers to a type of American Indian gathering that is common in Canada and the United States. At powwows, people of American Indian **heritage** meet to **socialize**, dance, sing and honor their cultures.

A powwow usually starts with a parade of dancers in colorful traditional clothing. The clothing has beautiful designs made with beads and feathers. Then there is singing and dancing to the beat of a drum. Later, there are dancing competitions for men and women. There are also stands where you can buy traditional food, such as grilled corn, **fry bread** and **venison** or **bison**. There are also modern snacks like hot dogs, pizza and lemonade.

Powwows can last for one day, or for up to a week if it is a special occasion. They can be at any time of the year. And they aren't just for American Indians—they're open to everyone. It's a great time to learn about different tribal cultures. There are a few rules you should follow if you go to a powwow: First, it's OK to wear regular clothes to a powwow. Please *don't* dress up like an "Indian." But please *do* wear clothing that is modest and respectful. Many powwows take place during the summer, but no swimsuits please! Lastly, remember to have fun! It's a celebration, after all!

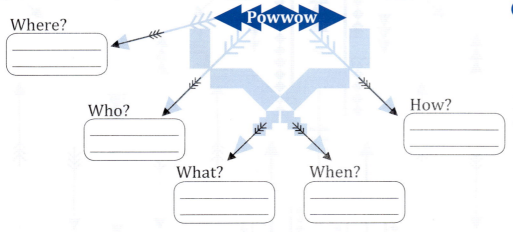

Glossary

gathering: an event with people from different places

heritage: ethnicity or culture

socialize: to talk to friends

fry bread: a flat dough fried in oil

venison: meat from deer

bison: buffalo meat

Vocabulary – First Aid

1 Look and complete.

0. first-aid kit
1. a_____ s_____
2. i_____ p_____
3. m_____
4. t_____
5. b_____
6. b_____ g_____

Symptoms and Injuries

2 Look, read and complete.

bruise   cut   fever   headache   runny nose   sore throat   stomachache   sunburn

0. Ouch! I have a cut on my finger.
1. 38 degrees. You have a _____.
2. Put on a hat or you'll get a _____.
3. I have a terrible _____.
4. Achoo! I have a _____.
5. Ugh. I have a really bad _____.
6. Oh, no. I'm going to have a _____ on my arm.
7. Do you have a _____?

Grammar – Should

1 Read and number the suggestions.

0 My sister has a bad cold. She has a runny nose and a sore throat.

1 My friends and I were at the beach and now we all have a bad sunburn!

2 My dad fell on some ice. Now he has a big bruise on his arm.

3 I got a paper cut. It's very small, but it hurts a lot!

4 I feel very hot and my face is red.

[ ] That's not good! You should try to avoid staying in the sun, but now that you have it, burn gel will help it to heal.

[ ] You should wash it, use antiseptic spray and put a bandage on it. It will heal in a day or two.

[0] I'm sorry to hear that. She should stay home and drink some hot tea.

[ ] Ouch! He should put an ice pack on it. It should get better soon.

[ ] Oh, you have a fever. You should check your temperature and then take some medicine.

Short Answers

Should I go to the doctor?
Yes, you **should**.
No, you **shouldn't**.

2 Complete the sentences using *should* or *shouldn't*.

0. You _____should_____ eat vegetables every day.
1. You _____ skip breakfast.
2. You _____ always wear a seatbelt.
3. You _____ avoid foods with a lot of sugar.
4. You _____ stay in the sun too long.

3 Unscramble and answer.

0. I / to / should / at / bed / midnight / go
   <u>Should I go to bed at midnight</u> ? <u>No, you shouldn't.</u>

1. for / junk food / should / eat / I / lunch
   _____ ? _____

2. I / my / wash / should / hands / before / dinner
   _____ ? _____

3. should / brush / teeth / I / my / night / at
   _____ ? _____

Unit 2

Zero Conditional

4 Read and underline the condition.

0. When <u>you lift weights</u>, you make your muscles stronger.
1. When kids eat a lot of junk food, they don't get enough nutrients.
2. People have trouble concentrating if they don't sleep well.
3. If I exercise regularly, I feel great.
4. Students feel more prepared when they study every night.

5 Read and match.

0. Life is less stressful if — you make your heart stronger.
1. You lose weight if — you have routines.
2. Your relationships suffer — your body doesn't function well.
3. When you exercise, — your body gets the right nutrients.
4. If you don't exercise, — when you spend too much time online.
5. You protect your teeth — you eat fewer calories.
6. When you eat a balanced diet, — when you brush them.

> **Zero Conditionals**
>
> We can also use negative forms in zero conditional sentences:
>
> If you **don't** eat fruits and vegetables, your body **doesn't** get important nutrients.

Review

1 Read and correct the sentences.

0. You should ~~to eat~~ a balanced diet.
   <u>You should eat a balanced diet.</u>
1. If you have a cold, your body need rest.
   _____
2. People shouldn't going to school when they are sick.
   _____
3. When you wash your hands you wash off viruses and bacteria.
   _____
4. If people see ads for junk food, they wanted to buy it.
   _____

Reading

1 Look and read. What is happening in the picture?

☐ The boy's pet is visiting him at the hospital.

☐ The dog has a job. It visits hospital **patients**.

☐ Doctors are treating the dog at the hospital.

2 Read and answer T (True) or F (False).

Animals Who Help

Animals and humans share a special connection. Animals make loyal companions, and some even work for humans. More and more, animals are participating in medical treatment to help patients. The use of these animals can improve a patient's physical, social and **cognitive** wellness. Therapy animals and service animals are two animal occupations where animals help humans to be healthy.

Therapy animals often visit hospitals or **nursing homes**. Patients receive many benefits: less pain and less fear—especially for children receiving medical treatment. Therapy animals can help patients to recover from severe injuries, manage **grief** after a traumatic event or find personal strength to overcome anxiety. Therapy animals help people to relax, smile, even laugh. Interacting with a therapy animal can even reduce a person's blood pressure. And animal therapy isn't just for dogs. There are also therapy horses, cats, birds and even fish. Many are pets with special training. They work with their owners to visit and encourage people.

Service animals are like therapy animals, except instead of visiting people, they live with patients. They are usually dogs, and they help people with a range of health conditions ranging from blindness to epilepsy. Some service dogs can guide a blind person through a busy neighborhood. Others can identify when a dangerous medical problem is about to occur or help a child with a physical disability to walk. Some service dogs help people with autism to **cope with** difficult situations. Service animals need a lot of training, and that training is specific to the need of their future owner. Because service animals are so important to the health and **well-being** of their humans, they can go anywhere: to stores, on planes—any place their person needs to go.

0. Therapy animals and service animals help humans to feel well.	(T)	F
1. Many different types of animals can be therapy animals.	T	F
2. Therapy animals only work in hospitals.	T	F
3. Service animals are pets that visit hospitals and nursing homes.	T	F
4. Service animals are usually dogs.	T	F
5. They are useful for different kinds of health conditions.	T	F
6. Service dogs can't go everywhere with their owners.	T	F

3 Complete the chart.

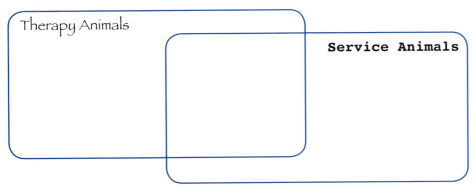

Glossary

patients: people who receive medical treatment

cognitive: related to the brain

nursing homes: places for people who need regular medical care

grief: sadness and loss, often after a death

cope with: to live and be well in spite of circumstances

well-being: health and happiness

Vocabulary – The Environment

1 Look and complete the sentences.

conserve   planting   ~~polluting~~   reducing   saves   send   use (x2)

It's _polluting_ the environment.

It _____ electricity.

They're _____ trees.

They _____ clean energy.

They _____ fossil fuels.

We _____ a lot of garbage to landfills.

Collecting rainwater is one way to _____ water.

_____ carbon emissions is important for the environment.

2 Correct the spelling errors.

0. fossil feuls — _fossil fuels_
1. elctricity _____
2. clean enerjy _____
3. garbidge _____
4. landfils _____
5. polution _____
6. envirenment _____

Grammar – First Conditional

1 Read and underline the consequence.

0. If people pick up after their dogs, <u>the city will be much cleaner</u>.
1. If people conserve water now, we will have enough water in the future.
2. We will pollute the environment more if we use a lot of electricity.
3. If we play loud music, we will bother our neighbors.
4. We will make our cities nicer if we plant more trees.
5. If we recycle, we will send less garbage to landfills.

2 Complete using the correct form of the verb.

0. If people don't pick up after their dogs, the city ____will be____ (be) very dirty.
1. If you _____ (listen) to very loud music, you will damage your ears.
2. If we don't control light pollution, we _____ (not be able) to see the stars.
3. If you take long showers, you _____ (use) a lot of water.
4. If we _____ (share) our cars, we will reduce our carbon footprint.
5. If we all work together, we _____ (make) a difference.

3 Read and switch the order of the condition and the consequence.

0. If we use regular lightbulbs, we will use more electricity.
   <u>We will use more electricity if we use regular lightbulbs.</u>
1. If we use cold water to wash clothes, we will save electricity.
   _____
2. If we don't use clean energy, we will change the Earth's climate.
   _____
3. Many animals will go extinct if the Earth's climate changes.
   _____

4 Look and write the questions. Then answer.

0. what / people / do … if / sea levels / rise / ?
   <u>What will people do if sea levels rise?</u>
   _____

1. where / people / live … if / cities / disappear underwater / ?
   _____
   _____

2. what / happen … if / many animals / go extinct / ?
   _____
   _____

3. how / we / grow food … if / bees / go extinct / ?
   _____
   _____

Unit 3

Review

1 Read and correct the sentences.

0. If we will use clean energy, we reduce our carbon footprint.
   If we use clean energy, we will reduce our carbon footprint.

1. If people doesn't conserve water, there won't be enough water in the future.
   _____

2. If there isn't enough water we won't be able to grow food.
   _____

3. We will change the climate if we doesn't reduce carbon emissions.
   _____

2 Answer about you.

1. Which activity is most important for your city or neighborhood? Why?
   planting trees   conserving water   picking up trash   recycling
   _____

2. List two things that you do to save electricity.
   _____
   _____

3. List two things that you do to conserve water.
   _____
   _____

3 Read the actions and write the impact they have on the environment.

0. I wear a sweater in the house when it is cold. → *You're saving electricity on heating.*

1. We use an electric car. → _____

2. We take our paper to a recycling center. → _____

3. I water my plants with a **bucket**, not a **hose**. → _____

4 Write two more similar exchanges.

1. _____ → _____

2. _____ → _____

Glossary

bucket: an open container with a handle used to carry water

hose: a flexible tube used to water plants, put out fires, etc.

Reading

1 Read quickly and answer. What requires the most water?

a) our food   b) home use   c) factory products

YOUR WATER FOOTPRINT

Every day, human beings use an enormous amount of water. On average, a person uses 130 liters of water at home to take a shower, **flush** the toilet, wash clothing and cook. We only drink a small amount, less than two liters. We use much more water—167 liters a day—in factories to make products such as paper, cotton and clothing. But the real surprise is that we use 3,496 liters of water for our food.

Why do we use so much water for food? Let's look at one example. To produce beef for hamburgers, we must provide food and water to a cow for three years. Just the food for the cow requires 3 million liters of water to grow. During its lifetime, the cow also drinks 24,000 liters of water. At the end of the process, for one kilo of beef, we use 15,400 liters of water—enough to fill a wall of water bottles 8 meters high and 40 meters wide.

What can we do about this situation? First of all, we can eat less meat, and when we *do* eat meat, we should choose meat from smaller animals like chickens. And remember other sources of protein like fish, eggs and soy. Second, we should drink less milk and eat less cheese. It is healthier to get nutrients from nuts and vegetables, and it uses less water. Finally, we can reduce food waste. In some countries, people throw away 30% of the food. Be sure to shop at farmer's markets and supermarkets that don't waste food just because it has imperfections—food that is good to eat, but has an unusual shape or color. Remember to wash and dry fresh fruits and vegetables and keep them in a cool, dry place. Use them before they **go bad**. And don't buy it if you aren't going to eat it.

Water is a vital resource, and one that we should protect. Reduce your water footprint today!

2 Read and underline the information. Write the amount.

0. the amount of water we use at home — 130 liters
1. the amount of water we drink — _____
2. the amount of water in factory products — _____
3. the amount of water to produce food — _____
4. the amount of water to produce 1 kg of beef — _____
5. the percent of food people throw away — _____

3 Decode the water footprint for each item (1=a, 2=b, etc.).

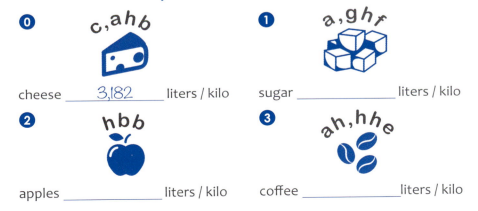

0 c,ahb cheese ____3,182____ liters / kilo

1 a,ghf sugar _____ liters / kilo

2 hbb apples _____ liters / kilo

3 ah,hhe coffee _____ liters / kilo

Unit 4

Vocabulary – Fan Activities

1 Look and complete the phrases.

0. put ___on___ face paint
1. wear a _____
2. _____ in line
3. put _____ posters
4. be good _____
5. dress up _____ characters
6. _____ an autograph
7. collect action _____
8. wear _____ colors
9. be a _____ of

2 Read and number.

0. We love jazz music. We listen to it all the time.
1. I waited for hours. There were a lot of people. Finally, I got a ticket to the concert.
2. My brother loves rock music. He has giant pictures of rock bands in his room.
3. Tomorrow is the big game. Remember your red and yellow T-shirts!
4. A famous athlete wrote his signature on my jersey.
5. She has a baseball cap for her favorite team. It's on her head.
6. We want to show that we are big fans, so we put bright colors on our faces.
7. She has more than one hundred superhero characters.
8. Some people think we're strange, but we love wearing costumes!
9. My brother can change his voice to talk like famous actors.

___0___ We're fans of jazz music.
_____ She collects action figures.
_____ I got his autograph!
_____ She's wearing a hat.
_____ We put on face paint.
_____ I stood in line.
_____ He's good at imitating actors' voices.
_____ We dress up as characters.
_____ Wear team colors.
_____ He puts up posters.

Grammar – Intensifiers

1 Number the intensifiers from least (0) to most intense (3).

_____ so/really   _____ pretty   _____ extremely   __0__ a bit

Intensifiers

Intensifiers are words that modify adjectives and adverbs:

The athlete is **extremely** fast.

She runs **pretty** fast.

2 Complete the dialogue using intensifiers.

MIKE: Hi, Gianna. Did you go to the Sci-Fi Festival yet?

GIANNA: No. I'm going this afternoon. How is it?

MIKE: It's (0) __really__ (!!!) cool. They have movies there, too. I watched *Planet of the Apes*. I didn't know sci-fi movies were (1) _____ (!!) entertaining. It was (2) _____ (!) long, though.

GIANNA: What else do they have at the festival?

MIKE: Well, the snacks and drinks are (3) _____ (!!) good. They have pepperoni pizza and chocolate chip cookies!

GIANNA: Did they have the costume contest yet?

MIKE: No, it's this afternoon.

GIANNA: Oh, good!

MIKE: You should see the fan art exhibition, too. Some of the artists are amazing! Their posters are (4) _____ (!!!!) realistic.

GIANNA: Cool! I can't wait!

Already, Yet

3 Look and circle the correct option.

0. Did they buy any snacks yet?
   (Yes, they did.) / No, they didn't.
1. Did they get into the festival yet?
   Yes, they did. / No, they didn't.
2. Did they already put on their costumes?
   Yes, they did. / No, they didn't.

Guess What!
It is also possible to use *already* in questions when we expect an affirmative answer: Did you **already** have lunch?

Unit 4

4 Read and circle T (True) or F (False).

0. We usually use *already* and *yet* to talk about the past.   (T)   F
1. We use *already* and *yet* with *Wh-* questions.   T   F
2. We use *already* and *yet* with *Yes-No* questions.   T   F
3. *Already* usually goes after the main verb in a sentence.   T   F
4. *Yet* always goes at the end of a sentence or question.   T   F

5 Unscramble and write.

0. get / you / yet / any / did / autographs / ?
   Did you get any autographs yet?
1. a / watch / did / yet / you / movie / ?
   _____
2. to / we / art / already / exhibition / went / the / .
   _____
3. already / registered / the / she / for / contest / .
   _____
4. have / did / already / you / some / snacks / ?
   _____

Review

1 Read and correct the sentences.

0. I'm a fan ~~for space movies~~.
   I'm a fan of space movies.
1. My friends and I dress up of characters.
   _____
2. My sister put on posters in her room.
   _____
3. For big games, we put up face paint.
   _____
4. Ryan is really good in dancing.
   _____
5. I stood at line for three hours.
   _____

2 Read and complete the sentences.

0. Sara ___already___ gave her presentation.
1. Max didn't see the art exhibition _____.
2. Did you make your costume _____?
3. Did you _____ have some snacks and drinks?
4. Lisa didn't see the movie _____.

Reading

1 Read and mark (✓) the topics in the article. Then circle the main idea of the article.

☐ famous players ☑ the number of fans ☐ the history of the club ☐ team colors ☐ rival teams
☐ sponsors ☐ the cost for fans ☐ video games ☐ how to watch a game

Real Madrid:
The World's Most Valuable Sports Team

The world's most valuable sports team is Real Madrid, a famous soccer club. The club dates to 1902, when soccer first became popular in Spain. Now, more than a **century** later, the team is worth $3.26 billion dollars. This is more than any other sports team in the world!

One reason the club is worth so much is because fans buy Real Madrid jerseys and other **merchandise**. And there are a lot of fans—450 million fans worldwide! There are fan clubs from Boston to Jakarta. Real Madrid also makes a lot of money from TV channels that broadcast their games. In addition, they receive money from **sponsors**. Real Madrid's sponsors include Audi, Adidas, Coca-Cola, Emirates Airlines and Microsoft. Adidas alone pays $800 million dollars a year in sponsorship.

Being a Real Madrid fan can be expensive. Tickets to a **home game** at Santiago Bernabéu Stadium in Madrid cost a minimum of $35 per person, but can be $250 or more. Many fans buy scarves, jerseys and hats with the team colors, white and gray. Some **devoted** fans go to **away games** in other cities in Spain or even other countries. Fans pay for the tickets and for travel expenses: airfare, hotels and taxis.

Of course you don't have to spend a fortune to be a *Madridista*—the name for a Real Madrid fan. You can always follow the team in the news or watch on TV. You can also pay to watch individual games online for about $10.

2 Read and match.

0. the value of the team — $3.26 billion dollars
1. Jakarta — the location of one fan club
2. Microsoft — a sponsor
3. white and gray — current team colors
4. Santiago Bernabéu — the name of a stadium
5. the minimum cost of a ticket — $35
6. the cost to watch a game online — $10

Glossary

century: 100 years

merchandise: things that a company sells

sponsors: companies that give money to support an athlete, team or organization

home game: a game in a team's home stadium

devoted: dedicated; loyal

away game: a game in another team's stadium

Unit 5

Vocabulary – Personal Experiences

1 Look, read and number.

You made a mistake. The result is 564, not 543.

Oh, no! I forgot it was his birthday! **0**

I saw it in the park and immediately fell in love with it.

I bought a lot of souvenirs there.

Stay on the trail. You don't want to get lost in the forest.

I think I am going to get in trouble…

Keepsakes

2 Find and circle names of five keepsakes.

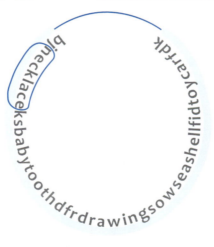

Guess What!
The words *foot*, *tooth* have irregular plural form: one tooth, two teeth; one foot, two feet

3 Complete the sentences using the words from Activity 2.

0. Emma Watson wore a long black dress and a diamond ____necklace____ to the award ceremony.

1. My mom has a jar full of _____. Mine, my sister's and my brother's. They are old and pretty ugly.

2. The _____ I made in preschool is still hanging on our refrigerator.

3. I love holding this _____ to my ear to hear the ocean.

4. My grandma still has that old _____ in the closet. She says I loved playing with it.

Grammar – Past Continuous

1 **Look and answer the questions.**

Yesterday at 10:10 a.m...

0. Was Alan paying attention?
   No, he wasn't.

1. Were Gina and Hal giving a presentation?
   _____

2. Was Miss Smith reading a book?
   _____

3. Were Claire, Emma and Pam sleeping?
   _____

4. Was Bill reading?
   _____

Short Answers

Was he drink**ing**?
Yes, he **was**. / No, he **wasn't**.

Were they eat**ing**?
Yes, they **were**. / No, they **weren't**.

Past Continuous: *While*

2 **Look again and write sentences using *while*.**

Yesterday at 10:10 a.m...

0. Gina and Hal / Miss Smith
   Gina and Hal were giving a presentation while Miss Smith was writing.

1. Alan / Bill
   _____

2. Miss Smith / Claire, Emma and Pam
   _____

3. Bill / Gina and Hal
   _____

Past Continuous and Past Simple: *When*

3 Write sentences using *when*.

0 do yoga

2 ride his bike

1 walk her dog

3 study for a math exam

0. earthquake start
   <u>She was doing yoga when the earthquake started.</u>

1. see an accident
   _____

2. his telephone ring
   _____

3. someone knock at the door
   _____

Review

1 Complete the table.

	Present Simple	Past Simple	Past Continuous
he	make a mistake	made a mistake	was making a mistake
they	get in trouble		
I		prepared breakfast	
she			was drinking
computer	works		
Dad		bought souvenirs	
they	have a lot of fun		

Reading

1 Read and underline two **hormones** that affect your body clock.

2 Read again and mark the times for each activity on the timeline.

   0. thinking creatively   1. having a light meal   2. sleeping
   3. doing exercise   4. having a short sleep

0	☐	☐	☐	☐
9:00 a.m. noon	3:00 p.m. 4:00 p.m.	6:00 p.m. 8:00 p.m.	8:00 p.m. 10:00 p.m.	10:00 p.m. 6:00 a.m.

Ring, ring! The alarm goes off. How are you feeling? Fresh and ready to go, or tired and **sluggish**? Believe it or not, there is a scientific explanation for this. Your body has an internal clock that marks the ideal times for your activities and rest. Let's check it out!

Your Body Clock

The moment you wake up, the production of the sleep hormone, melatonin, stops. The best time to do it is around 6 a.m. To feel fully awake, go out to direct light as soon as you wake up. If you have a dog, walk it—you will feel awake immediately. Between 9:00 a.m. and noon, your mind is at its maximum level of alertness. At this time of the day, the stress hormone, cortisol, keeps your brain active. It's a good time to be creative. And to have a math class!

The best time to have a big meal of the day is around 3 p.m. Is this when you finish school? If so, you must feel very hungry. Eat and let your body **digest** the food. And maybe take a short nap!

From 6:00 to 8:00 p.m. your body temperature increases, your **heart** and **lungs** work better and your muscles are 6% stronger than at other times of the day. As a result, this is a great time to do exercise. Go to the gym, run around the park or simply jump rope! Any exercise is fine as long as you do it regularly.

In the evening, the brain produces melatonin to make you sleepy. Don't eat heavy meals after 8 p.m. Your digestion is much slower in the evening and you can easily gain weight. Don't look at bright screens on tablets or phones because the light can change your body chemistry and make it hard to fall asleep. As the melatonin takes effect, your body temperature goes down and you'll feel like going to bed. From 10 p.m. to 6:00 a.m., the brain is cleaning out the waste **toxins** from a hard day of thinking.

So, is this what your day is like?

3 **Think Fast!** In your notebook, draw a timeline about your day.

Glossary

hormone: natural substance that controls activities in the body

sluggish: not alert, slow in movement

digest: process food in the stomach

heart:

lungs:

toxins: poisonous substances that cause disease

Unit 6

Vocabulary – Travel

1 Unscramble and match. Then look and number the photos.

0. hxeangce ____exchange____ — a guide
1. irhe _____ — a suitcase
2. yast _____ — in a hotel
3. okob _____ — a flight
4. chatc _____ — a passport
5. teg _____ — a train
6. capk _____ — money

Collocations

2 Read and complete the sentences.

0. My sister gets _____angry_____ when I ask her to wash the dishes.
1. I get very _____ when I exercise, so I always carry a bottle of water.
2. My brother always gets _____ late—and he sets three alarms!
3. My sister is on a diet, but it's difficult because she gets _____ very quickly.
4. I have to get _____ for the math exam next week.
5. I look forward to my vacation in Hawaii. When I get _____, I'm going straight to the beach.
6. My aunt gets _____ every time she visits the city. I'm going to buy her a GPS.
7. If I'm going to finish this homework, I need to get _____ soon.

Grammar – Present Perfect

1 Read and complete using *ever* and the present perfect.

0. (*be*) <u>Have you ever been to China?</u>
   Yes, I have. I went to China in 2015.
1. (*try chai tea*) _____
   Yes, he has. He tried chai tea in India.
2. (*get lost*) _____
   Yes, she has. She got lost in the mountains last summer.
3. (*take a train*) _____
   Yes, they have. They took a train in Europe.
4. (*live abroad*) _____
   Yes, I have. I lived in Italy for a year.

Short Answers

When you ask about life experiences using *ever*, you use the present perfect. When you want to specify the exact moment you did something, you use the past simple:

Has he **been** to South Africa?

No, he **hasn't**.

Have you ever **eaten** curry?

Yes, I **have**. I **ate** curry in India.

Guess What!

In American English, the past participle of got is gotten: *Has she ever gotten lost?* Other past participle forms are the same as the past simple forms: *tried, traveled, lived, had.*

2 Look and write sentences using *already* and *yet*.

0. <u>I have already seen a family of elephants.</u>
1. _____
2. _____
3. _____
4. _____
5. _____
6. _____

Things to do:
- see a family of elephants ✓
- take pictures ✓
- watch a sunset ✓
- eat bobotie ✗
- give monkey bananas ✗
- buy souvenirs ✗
- hear a lion roar ✓

Unit 6

3 Read and circle the correct option.

0. Have you **(been)** / gone to the supermarket?
   Yes, I I bought some chocolates.
1. Have you **been** / **gone** to the new mall?
   No, not yet.
2. Has he **been** / **gone** to France? Yes, he's enjoying every moment of his trip!
3. Have they **been** / **gone** on vacation? Yes, they're staying at a hotel near the beach.
4. Has she **been** / **gone** to the movies? Yes, she loved the movie.

Been, Gone

We can use *been* and *gone* to talk about visiting a place, but there is a difference in meaning:
Have you **been** to New Zealand?
Yes, I have. (This means you are not there now.)
Has he **gone** to London?
Yes, he has. (This means he is there now.)

Review

1 Read and complete the e-mail.

hot   hungry   lost   ready   started   ~~there~~   thirsty   up

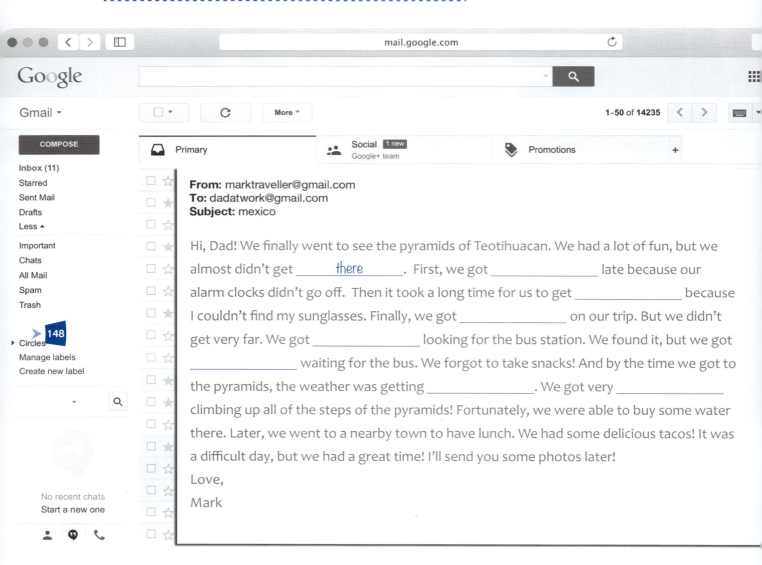

From: marktraveller@gmail.com
To: dadatwork@gmail.com
Subject: mexico

Hi, Dad! We finally went to see the pyramids of Teotihuacan. We had a lot of fun, but we almost didn't get ____there____. First, we got _____ late because our alarm clocks didn't go off. Then it took a long time for us to get _____ because I couldn't find my sunglasses. Finally, we got _____ on our trip. But we didn't get very far. We got _____ looking for the bus station. We found it, but we got _____ waiting for the bus. We forgot to take snacks! And by the time we got to the pyramids, the weather was getting _____. We got very _____ climbing up all of the steps of the pyramids! Fortunately, we were able to buy some water there. Later, we went to a nearby town to have lunch. We had some delicious tacos! It was a difficult day, but we had a great time! I'll send you some photos later!

Love,

Mark

Reading

1 Look at the map and circle the correct option.

0. It's a map of **Saudi Arabia** / **India**.
1. Kanyakumari and Dibrugarh are small **islands** / **cities**.
2. The line represents a **railway** / **river**.
3. The article is probably about **shopping** / **transportation**.

2 Read the article and match the numbers with their meaning.

The Longest Train

Have you ever been on a train? An easy question? Well, let me rephrase it…

Have you ever spent more than 80 hours on the same train? No? Maybe it is time for an adventure, then!

Railways in India date back to 1848, when British colonists realized there was a great need to connect the different parts of this huge country. Now the railway system has grown so much that India has one of the biggest railway networks in the world—just enough to provide service for India's 1.2 billion people!

Selling snacks

So, let's board the Dibrugarh-Kanyakumari Vivek Express! Indian Railway number 15906 is the longest train line in India, both in terms of travel time and distance. During your trip, you will cover a distance of 4,281 km in 3 days, 11 hours and 5 minutes. Yes, that's right! You will leave on a Saturday night from Dibrugarh station in the northeastern state of Assam, the land of tea-growers, and you will arrive in Kanyakumari, in the buzzing business-oriented state of Tamil Nadu on Wednesday morning. You will be traveling on a 21-car train in company of 1,800 other passengers!

Admiring the view

You should also know that there are different classes of cars on your train. If you are a poor student, you can't afford the air-conditioned cars with beds, which cost around $60 per person. You can get a ticket on a sleeper car without air conditioning, but if you really want to save money, or you can't book your ticket in advance, you have only one option: unreserved. There are no beds—just wooden benches if you are the first one to arrive. If you arrive late, you can sit on the floor or hang in a hammock. It's the perfect solution for a poor student at only $9.

Now that you're on the train, what can you do during your three-and-a-half-day trip? Take photographs, read—or simply shop! You will see a lot of people at railway stations selling everything you can imagine: candy and peanuts, fingernail scissors and pens, samosas and bananas—but most of all *chai*, tea with milk, sugar and sometimes spices. You can have hundreds of tiny cups of chai in all the hours to come!

Samosas and chai

Enjoy your trip! India's beauty will amaze you.

____ number of passengers ____ the price of a ticket in an air-conditioned car with a bed

____ the population of India _0_ the beginning of construction of railways in India

____ the distance of the trip ____ the railway number ____ the number of train cars

Unit 7

Vocabulary – Extreme Sports

1 Read and match to form extreme sports.

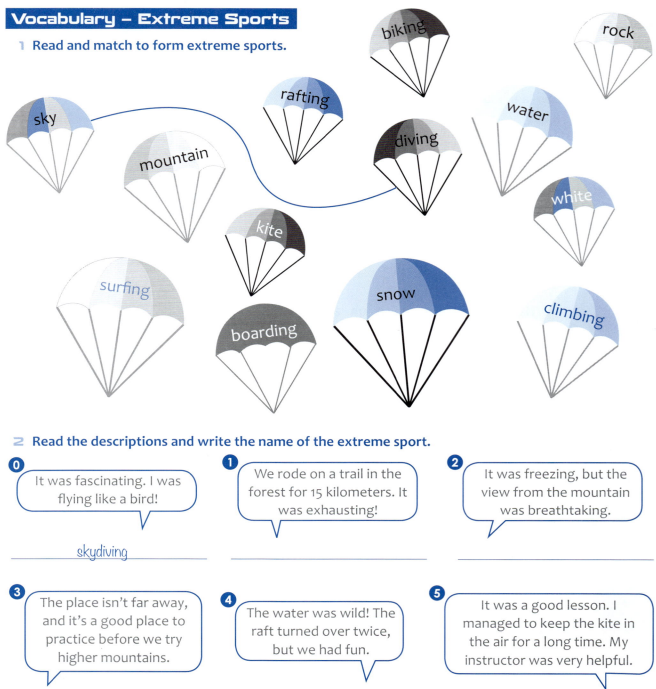

2 Read the descriptions and write the name of the extreme sport.

0. It was fascinating. I was flying like a bird!
   skydiving

1. We rode on a trail in the forest for 15 kilometers. It was exhausting!
   _____

2. It was freezing, but the view from the mountain was breathtaking.
   _____

3. The place isn't far away, and it's a good place to practice before we try higher mountains.
   _____

4. The water was wild! The raft turned over twice, but we had fun.
   _____

5. It was a good lesson. I managed to keep the kite in the air for a long time. My instructor was very helpful.
   _____

Adjectives

3 Circle the correct option.

0. I am **terrified** / terrifying of heights.
1. The experience of hiking in the mountains was **thrilled / thrilling**.
2. The radio presenter was so **bored / boring** that I fell asleep.
3. I was **tired / tiring** after the bike ride.
4. The rollercoaster wasn't as **excited / exciting** as I hoped.
5. She was very **interested / interesting** in his speech.

Grammar – Might

1 Look and write sentences using *might*.

0. (take / compass) I might take a compass.
1. (take photos) _____
2. (run / 10 km) _____
3. (visit / Butterfly Sanctuary) _____
4. (get thirsty) _____
5. (wear / life jacket) _____

Would

> **Guess What!**
> We use *would* for hypothetical situations in the future.

2 Unscramble the sentences. Then look and number the situations.

0. never / would / him / I / party / invite / to / a I would never invite him to a party.
1. in / Would / train / by / Europe / you / travel _____
2. live / Canada / We / in / would / never _____
3. jungle adventure / a / she / ever / go / Would / trip / on _____
_____
4. go / would / She / skydiving / never _____

He is so boring!

She's terrified of heights.

The tickets are so expensive.

Unit 7

Present Perfect: *Never*

3 Look and complete using the present perfect and *never*.

0

Have you ever baked a birthday cake?

No, I __haven't__.
I __'ve never baked__ a birthday cake.

1

Have you ever gone diving in the Indian Ocean?

No, I _____.
I _____ in the Indian Ocean.

2

Have they ever flown in a helicopter?

No, they _____.
They _____ in a helicopter.

3

Has she ever sung karaoke?

No, she _____.
She _____ karaoke.

4

Has he ever gone skydiving?

No, he _____.
He _____ skydiving.

5

Have they ever been to France?

No, they _____.
They _____ to France.

Review

1 Read and complete the sentences using participle adjectives.

0. This is a boring movie. I am __bored__.
1. She is interested in the topic. The topic is _____.
2. The adventure was thrilling. All the participants felt _____.
3. The news was _____. Everybody was excited.
4. I felt tired. The trip to the forest was really _____.
5. The encounter with the bear was terrifying. We were _____.

Reading

1 Read the article and underline the adjectives that don't describe Bethany.

<u>boring</u>   determined   inspiring   lucky   brave   disabled   unprofessional   terrifying

2 Read again and underline the following information.

0. Bethany's last name   1. the day of the accident   2. the name of her friend
3. the title of the movie   4. her latest competition   5. meaning of "wildcard"

Soul Surfer

ABOUT   CONNECT WITH GOD   GALLERY

Bethany <u>Hamilton</u> was born in Hawaii on February 8, 1990. Both her parents were surfers, so she was introduced to surfing at a very young age. She began competing at the age of eight and at 11 she won the Haleiwa Menehune competition in two categories. After the competition, she was offered a **sponsorship** and she started to **pursue** her professional **career**.

October 31, 2003 was just like any other morning for Bethany. She woke up early, and by 7:30 a.m. she was already on the beach with her surfboard. She was with her friend Alana, Alana's father and Alana's brother. The ocean was calm, so they got into the water to paddle on their boards, waiting for the waves to **pick up**. Bethany was lying on her surfboard with her arms in water when suddenly she felt a tremendous pressure on her left arm. At first, she didn't feel any pain, but she was terrified when she saw the water near her turn red. In a matter of seconds, her friends realized that a tiger shark had attacked Bethany. Her left arm was gone. Alana's father quickly made a **tourniquet** using his surfboard leash, got everyone out of the water and got Bethany to the hospital. In spite of losing 60% of her blood, Bethany survived.

Bethany was back in the water only a month after the shark attack. Her amazing recovery was a result of passion, determination and **faith**. Later, she won several competitions—proving that a loss of arm was not an obstacle to fulfilling her surfing goals. Inspired by her story, the movie *Soul Surfer* was released in 2011.

Bethany Hamilton appeared in the news again in 2016 when she participated in and won third place in a World Surf League's Fiji Woman's Pro competition. She entered as a wildcard, which means she wasn't considered a top surfer. She is a great example of an athlete whose passion cannot be stopped by any adversity. Nowadays, Bethany is still living in Hawaii with her husband and her son, Tobias.

Glossary

soul: a spiritual part of a person

sponsorship: money an organization pays someone in exchange for the right to advertise

pursue: to try to get or do something over a period of time

career: a job of profession

pick up: to gradually increase

tourniquet: a bandage, strip of cloth, etc., that is tied around an injured body part to slow the bleeding

faith: strong belief

8 Unit

Vocabulary – Habits

1 Decode the names of habits. Then number the photos.

0. w o r k o u t
1. ☐☐☐☐ ☐ ☐☐☐☐☐☐☐
2. ☐☐ ☐☐☐ ☐☐ ☐☐☐
3. ☐☐☐☐ ☐☐
4. ☐☐☐☐☐ ☐☐☐☐-☐☐☐
5. ☐☐☐☐☐
6. ☐☐☐☐ ☐☐ ☐☐☐☐
7. ☐☐☐☐☐ ☐☐☐☐☐☐

Grammar – Too, Either

1 Unscramble and write.

0. hate / papaya / I
   I hate papaya.
   I do too.

1. she / sleeps in / often
   _____
   (he) _____

2. every day / work out / don't / I
   _____
   (she) _____

3. can't / today / with / she / hang out / them
   _____
   (I) _____

4. is / our / cool / teacher / English
   _____
   (math teacher) _____

5. with / happy / aren't / results / they / the football
   _____
   (we) _____

So, Neither

2 Read and number the lines of the dialogue.

Tom: So did I. What did you think? ☐

Natalia: Yes, I did. I streamed it live on my computer. ☐

Natalia: I don't want to talk about it either! ☐

Natalia: It was horrible. I thought they were going to win. ☐

Tom: Did you see the game last night? [0]

Tom: So did I. Then, at the last second, the other team scored a goal. ☐

Natalia: I feel sad for all the fans. ☐

Tom: So do I. But I don't want to talk about it anymore. ☐

Unit 8

3 **Write a dialogue for each photo.**

> **Guess What!**
> It's common in spoken English to show agreement with the expression *Me too*, or for agreement with negative statements, *Me neither*. They mean the same as *So do I* and *Neither do I*.

0. I'm hungry.
1. _____
2. _____

Me too!

Review

1 **Look and write a paragraph about their habits.**

Are Jo and Elsie similar or different?

0. Jo orders take-out. Elsie goes out to eat. _____
_____
_____
_____

Reading

1 Read and classify the adjectives.

casual energetic hardworking honest
lonely old retired stressed talented

Unlikely Friendships

It's often the case that people choose friends who are like them in age, character and style. But in movies, there are often unlikely relationships between people who are appear to have nothing in common. In the 2015 comedy *The Intern,* Ben Whittaker (played by Robert De Niro) is a 70-year-old **widower** who is lonely at home and bored with **retirement**. He decides to apply for a job in a successful e-commerce clothing company owned by energetic and talented—but stressed—**entrepreneur** Jules Ostin (played by Ann Hathaway). Ben, whose previous job experience was selling telephone directories, gets the position. He shows up to work wearing a suit and a tie. Everyone else there wears casual clothes. At first, everyone at the company ignores him, but they soon learn that he's honest and hardworking, and has some valuable ideas to contribute.

The movie works well because two very different people find out that they can learn from each other—and that they do have things in common. In the end, it doesn't **matter** that they are from different generations with different views about life. It's possible to respect, like and learn from people who are different.

2 Read, match and complete.

0. Why does Ben apply for the job?
1. What does Jules Ostin do?
2. How old is Ben?
3. What does the company sell?
4. What do the main characters learn?

a. She's the owner of an _____ company.
b. He's _____ years old.
c. They have things in _____.
d. He is ___retired___ and lonely.
e. They sell _____ online.

Glossary
widower: a man whose wife has died
retirement: a stage in later life when a person doesn't work
entrepreneur: a person who starts his/her own business
matter: to be important

Just for Fun Answer Key

Unit 1
1 Halloween, Independence Day, Valentine's Day, Thanksgiving
2 *Down*: 1. Catrina 2. candles 3. turkey 4. present; *Across*: 5. diploma 6. cap 7. resolutions 8. celebrations

Unit 2
1 1. F – It takes two hours! 2. T 3. T 4. F – You burn about one calorie per kilogram of body weight per hour of sleep. 5. T 6. F – It takes less than 12 hours. 7. F – It's 25%. 8. T
2 Row 1: 1, 6, 8, 4
Row 2: 5, 2, 7, 3

Unit 3
1 If you turn off the water when you wash your hair, you will save up to 500 liters per month!
Buy a cloth bag and use it when you shop. If you stop using plastic bags, you will keep them out of landfills—and prevent them from polluting the environment.
If you eat chicken instead of beef, you can reduce your carbon footprint by 500%!
You don't need to buy solar panels to use clean energy. If you use natural sunlight instead of a lamp, you won't need any electricity or use any fossil fuels!
Planting trees helps the environment, but all plants do! If you keep a small plant in your house, it will produce oxygen and clean the air.
2 Row 1: 1, 3, 2, 3
Row 2: 1, 2, 3, 2

Unit 4
Kylie collects action figures; Olivia is a fan of a team; Will collects athletes' autographs; Jake collects movie posters; Max dresses up as video game characters

Unit 5
1 earthquake p. 73; lifeguards p. 72; neurons p. 74; reef p. 77; toy car p. 71
2 his grandpa; coffee; their uncle; network; Uluru
3 The lifeguard had hiccups. The waiter broke the glass to frighten him and cure the hiccups.

Unit 6
1

2 1. angry 2. bored 3. cold 4. full 5. tired 6. wet

Unit 7
1 1. rock climbing 2. mountain biking 3. kite surfing 4. snowboarding 5. skydiving 6. white water rafting
2 Column 1: terrifying, thrilling, tiring
Column 3: excited, terrified, bored, interested

Unit 8
1 Answers will vary.

Grammar Reference

Unit 1

Present Continuous (future meaning)

We usually use the present continuous to talk about actions that are happening now. However, we can also use it to talk about future plans. We form the present continuous with the verb *be* in the present simple, and the base form of the verb with *-ing*.

- I **am marching** in the parade tomorrow.
- The city **is setting off** fireworks tonight.
- We **are celebrating** her birthday on Saturday.

We usually use contractions with the present continuous.

- I**'m marching** in the parade tomorrow.
- The city**'s setting off** fireworks tonight.
- We**'re celebrating** her birthday on Saturday.

Remember that some verbs require spelling changes. We double the consonant in verbs with a short vowel sound that end in a consonant.

- He's **getting** his diploma this afternoon. (get)

We remove the *–e* and add *–ing* to verbs with a long vowel that end in *–e*.

- We're **making** resolutions at midnight. (make)

We form the negative by adding *not* after the verb *be*.

- She is **not** baking a pie for Thanksgiving.
- They are **not** opening their presents before Christmas.

Most people use the contracted form.

- She **isn't** baking a pie for Thanksgiving.
- They **aren't** opening their presents before Christmas.

To form *Yes/No* questions, we put the verb *be* before the subject. We don't use the main verb in short answers.

- **Is** he coming to visit later?
- Yes, he **is**. / No, he **isn't**.

For *Wh-* questions, we add a question word at the beginning.

- **When** are they arriving?
- After lunch.

Unit 2

Should

We use the modal *should* to give advice and recommendations. We use the base form of the main verb after a modal.

- You **should eat** a lot of vegetables.

We form the negative by adding *not* after the modal *should*. It is more common to use the contracted form.

- We **should not** drink a lot of soda.
- We **shouldn't** drink a lot of soda.

Zero Conditional

We use the zero conditional to express facts. There are two parts of a zero conditional sentence: the condition and the consequence. The condition begins with the word *if* or *when*. When the condition comes before the consequence, there is a comma after the condition.

- **If** you eat well**,** you feel better.
- **When** you eat well**,** you feel better.

The order of the condition and the consequence can be reversed. When the condition comes after the consequence, there is no comma.

- You feel better **if** you eat well.
- You feel better **when** you eat well.

Both the condition and the consequence use the present simple tense.

- You **sleep** better when you **don't use** a tablet before bed.

Unit 3

First Conditional

We use the first conditional to talk about future possibilities. The condition begins with the word *if* and the verb in the condition is in the present simple. We use *will* and the base form of the verb in the consequence.

- *If we **use** clean energy, there **will be** less pollution.*

As with all conditionals, the order of the condition and the consequence can be reversed.

- *There **will be** less pollution if we **use** clean energy.*

We form negative conditions by adding *don't* before the main verb.

- *If we **don't** recycle, there will be too much garbage.*

We form negative consequences by adding *won't* before the main verb.

- *If we pollute the environment, future generations **won't** have clean air or water.*

We can also form questions with conditionals.

- *If I use modern lightbulbs, **will I save** electricity?*

- ***What will happen** if I listen to loud music?*

Unit 4

Intensifiers

We use intensifiers to express the intensity of an adjective.

- It was **extremely** difficult to plan the party.
- His costume is **so** cool.
- Your collection is **really** interesting.
- His last album was **pretty** good.
- I'm running **a bit** late.

Intensifiers express a range of intensity.

extremely	→	!!!!
so	→	!!!
really	→	!!!
pretty	→	!!
a bit	→	!

Already, Yet

We use the adverbs *already* and *yet* to talk about our expectations regarding the time of an activity. In general, we use *already* in affirmative sentences. We use *yet* in negative sentences and questions. We can use *already* and *yet* with any tense. In American English, it is common to use it with the past simple.

- The store was **already** closed.
- We didn't register for the conference **yet**.
- Did they have lunch **yet**?

We use *already* in a different part of the sentence than *yet*. *Already* comes after *be* or before a main verb, similar to the word *not*.

- They are **already** late.
- We **already** saw that movie.

We use *yet* at the end of a sentence or question.

- We didn't finish our project **yet**.
- Did you do your homework **yet**?

We can sometimes use *already* in questions, to express that we expect an affirmative answer.

- Did he **already** do his homework?

Unit 5

Past Continuous

We usually use the past continuous to talk about actions that were happening over a period of time in the past. We use the past form of the verb *be* and the base form of the verb with *-ing*.

- I **was studying** at the library.
- They **were playing** soccer at the park.

Remember that some verbs require spelling changes. We double the consonant in verbs with a short vowel sound that end in a consonant.

- He was **swimming** near the shore. (swim)

We remove the *–e* and add *–ing* to verbs with a long vowel that end in *–e*.

- She was **taking** photos of the sunset. (take)

We form the negative by adding *not* after the verb *be*.

- She was **not** waiting at the school.
- They were **not** eating dinner.

Most people use the contracted form.

- She **wasn't** waiting at the school.
- They **weren't** eating dinner.

Past Continuous: *While*

We use *while* and two past continuous clauses together to express that two ongoing activities occurred simultaneously.

- She **was sending texts while** she **was studying**.

Past Continuous and Past Simple: *When*

We use the past continuous together with the past simple to express that an ongoing activity was interrupted by another activity.

- The family **was swimming** when strong currents **pulled** them away from the beach.

The word *when* goes before the past simple clause of the sentence.

- The family was swimming **when strong currents pulled them away from the beach.**

Present Perfect

We use the present perfect to talk about achievements and experiences. We use the present simple form of *have* and the past participle of the main verb.

- She **has been** to Hawaii twice.
- They **have climbed** a volcano.

Past participles can be regular or irregular. Past participles are included on the *Verb List* on page 168.

We form the negative by adding *not* after the verb *have*. Contractions are more common.

- I **haven't** been to Hawaii before.
- He **hasn't** won any awards.

Ever

We usually use *ever* to ask about achievements and experiences.

- Have you **ever** been to England?

We can use short answers with the present perfect.

- Have you ever been to England?
- Yes, I have.
- No, I haven't.

Already, Yet

We can use also use *already* and *yet* with the present perfect.

- They have **already** made some friends.
- Has she done anything interesting **yet**?

Unit 7

Might

We use the modal *might* before verbs to indicate possibility.

- I **might** take a survival course.

The negative form also indicates possibility, or doubt that something will happen.

- I **might not** sign up this year.

As with other modals, we always use the base form of the main verb with *might*.

Would

We use *would* for hypothetical situations in the future. It is common in questions. We can answer with short answers.

- **Would** you eat a bug?
- Yes, I **would**.
- No, I **wouldn't**.

Present Perfect: *Never*

We use *never* in combination with the present perfect to emphasize that an experience has not happened at any time in the past. This is a variation of the negative form. As with *not*, *never* goes after *have* and before the past participle.

- I've **never** eaten a bug.
- He's **never** learned to swim.

Unit 8

Too, Either

We can express similar opinions or circumstances using *too* and *either*. We use *too* at the end of affirmative sentences.
- *I like sushi.*
- *I like sushi* **too**.

We use *either* at the end of negative sentences to express similar opinions or circumstances.
- *He doesn't watch TV.*
- *I don't watch TV* **either**.

So, Neither

We can also use expressions with *So* and *Neither* to express similar opinions or circumstances. With most verbs, we use the auxiliary *do* in the expression. We use *So* with affirmative sentences.
- *I* **have** *a headache.*
- *So* **do** *I.*

We use *Neither* with negative sentences. With negative sentences, the word *Neither* eliminates the need for *not*.
- *I* **don't** *have a calculator.*
- *Neither* **do** *I.*

We use *be* to express agreement with sentences with *be* as a main verb or an auxiliary verb.
- *I'm a big fan of Formula 1 racing.*
- *So* **am** *I.*
- *We're studying for the math exam.*
- *So* **are** *we.*
- *They* **aren't** *going to the movies.*
- **Neither** *are we.*

Modals like *can, should* and *would* are also used in these expressions.
- *I* **can** *run a kilometer in six minutes.*
- *So* **can** *I.*
- *You* **should** *drink more water.*
- *So* **should** *you.*
- *I* **wouldn't** *eat a bug.*
- *Neither* **would** *I.*

Me too, Me neither

It's common in spoken English to express similar opinions or circumstances with the expression *Me too*, or for negative sentences, *Me neither*.
- *I like dancing.*
- **Me too**.
- *He doesn't watch TV.*
- **Me neither**.

Verb List

Base Form	Past Simple	Past Participle	Base Form	Past Simple	Past Participle
become	became *	become	include	included	included
begin	began	begun	invent	invented	invented
believe	believed	believed	keep	kept	kept
blow out	blew out	blown out	laugh	laughed	laughed
book	booked	booked	learn	learned	learned
break	broke	broken	leave	left	left
build	built	built	make	made	made
burn	burned	burnt	open	opened	opened
buy	bought	bought	order	ordered	ordered
catch	caught	caught	pack	packed	packed
cause	caused	caused	paint	painted	painted
celebrate	celebrated	celebrated	plant	planted	planted
change	changed	changed	pollute	polluted	polluted
check	checked	checked	practice	practiced	practiced
collect	collected	collected	prevent	prevented	prevented
come	came	come	produce	produced	produced
complete	completed	completed	protect	protected	protected
conserve	conserved	conserved	provide	provided	provided
cry	cried	cried	put	put	put
dance	danced	danced	reach	reached	reached
decorate	decorated	decorated	receive	received	received
draw	drew	drawn	recycle	recycled	recycled
dress	dressed	dressed	reduce	reduced	reduced
drink	drank	drunk	relax	relaxed	relaxed
drop	dropped	dropped	remember	remembered	remembered
eat	ate	eaten	reuse	reused	reused
escape	escaped	escaped	save	saved	saved
exchange	exchanged	exchanged	say	said	said
exercise	exercised	exercised	see	saw	seen
explore	explored	explored	send	sent	sent
fall	fell	fallen	sleep in	slept in	slept in
feed	fed	fed	start	started	started
feel	felt	felt	stay up	stayed up	stayed up
find	found	found	stream	streamed	streamed
get	got	gotten	take	took	taken
give	gave	given	teach	taught	taught
go	went	gone	throw	threw	thrown
hang out	hung out	hung out	try	tried	tried
happen	happened	happened	turn	turned	turned
have	had	had	wave	waved	waved
hear	heard	heard	wear	wore	worn
hire	hired	hired	work out	worked out	worked out
improve	improved	improved	write	wrote	written

* Irregular verbs